DISCOVERING THE
Fullness of
Worship

by
Paul E. Engle

GREAT COMMISSION PUBLICATIONS

To Margie,
my partner in discovering
the fullness of worship.

ISBN 0-934688-01-X

Seventh printing

Printed in USA

Published by Great Commission Publications
3640 Windsor Park Drive, Suite 100
Suwanee, GA 30024-3897

TABLE OF CONTENTS

1

Worship Under the
Old Covenant

1

HE TOOK THE INITIATIVE

This chapter shows how worship is based on God's initiative in revealing his name, his glory, and his attributes and acts—all of which call forth worship.

Have you ever caught yourself daydreaming in a church service? Have you ever struggled to keep your head from nodding? If so, perhaps you were brought back to reality by a gentle elbow in the ribs from the person next to you. It may be that the Sunday morning worship service is not the most exciting hour of the week for you. You may even wonder why you bother to attend. Something is wrong and you know it, but you seem unable to do anything to improve your situation.

A recent television newscast showed hundreds of young people standing in line. It was seven o'clock in the morning on a frigid winter day. A well-known rock group was scheduled to appear in concert. So hundreds of young people rose early and stood in the cold to purchase concert tickets. It is not often that one sees among Christians that same kind of motivation to enter God's presence in a service of worship.

One of the most serious needs in the church today is the rediscovery of biblical worship. Many church leaders recognize this and are calling the church to a renewed concern for worship. Robert Webber has pointed out the gravity of the problem in the following quote:

The area in which the least reform has taken place among us is in our corporate worship life. Through an unofficial survey, I discovered that the majority of evangelical lay people don't have the foggiest notion of what corporate worship really is. To questions such as: Why does God want to be worshiped? What is the meaning of an invocation or benediction? What does reading the Scripture, praying or hearing a sermon have to do with worship? I received blank stares and bewildered looks.

This statement, which appeared in a monthly evangelical magazine, concluded, "Part of the problem is that we have made our churches into centers of evangelism and instruction. The focus of our services is on man and his needs instead of God and his glory."[1]

The rediscovery of God-centered worship must come from a fresh examination of the biblical teaching concerning worship. The Bible is the book of worship *par excellence*. What, then, does it teach us about this purpose for which we were created?

One thing the Bible clearly teaches is that *worship depends on knowing the self-revealing God*. Proper worship would have been impossible if God had not taken the initiative to make himself known. This is a basic principle of worship that can be illustrated from the Old Testament.

GOD TOOK THE INITIATIVE
TO REVEAL HIS NAME

Some parents are highly selective in choosing a name for their son or daughter. They may look through long lists to find the name that's most appropriate. The ancient Hebrews were also selective in the choosing of names. They regarded a name as a reflection of a person's character. A person's name became interchangeable with the person himself.

This helps us appreciate the high regard which the Hebrews had for God's name. They believed the divine name was inseparably related to God's very being and character. Thus his name was greatly revered. This was especially true of the Hebrew consonants JHWH representing the name Jehovah or Yahweh. The Hebrews refused to pronounce those sacred consonants. The word *Adonai* meaning "Lord" was used in its place. The King James Version reflects this usage in its translation of JHWH as "Lord" throughout the Old Testament.

God's revelation of himself to men often involved the use of his name. He appeared to Jacob (Genesis 35:11) and said, "I am the God Almighty" (*El-Shaddai*). God revealed himself to Moses (Exodus 6:2) saying, "I am the Lord" (*Yahweh*). To reveal his name was for God to reveal himself. This divine self-revelation led to worship. Once people knew God's name they used it to invoke his presence for worship. The first reference to public worship is in Genesis 4:26 — "people began to call upon the name of the Lord." This same expression is repeated elsewhere in the book of Genesis.

God not only revealed his name but he attached his name to symbolic dwelling places, places where he was present in a special way. Worship occurred in these locations during the Old Testament period. God's name was connected with certain altars. He commanded, "You shall make an altar of earth for Me, and . . .in every place where I cause My name to be remembered, I will come to you and bless you" (Exodus 20:24). He likewise placed his name at Jerusalem (I Kings 11:36) and at Shiloh (Jeremiah 7:12). Consequently, these cities became centers of worship where people assembled to call on the name of the Lord.

Have you noticed the frequent use of the divine names in services of public worship today? In some churches the minister begins the service with a salutation in God's name: "Grace to you and peace from God our Father and the Lord Jesus Christ." Prayers are addressed to the Father with the help of the Holy Spirit in the name of our Lord Jesus Christ. Worship services often conclude with a benediction using the names of the triune God.

The use of divine names in worship has significance. God's being and God's presence are reflected in the very use of the names. When you participate in the worship service, listen for this and be prepared to worship just as the children of Israel did.

GOD TOOK THE INITIATIVE TO REVEAL HIS GLORY

Worship depends on knowing the self-revealing God who has taken the initiative to reveal his glory. This glory was revealed to Israel on various occasions. The first place in which it was seen was Mount Sinai. The Israelites had been freed from slavery in Egypt. They crossed the Red Sea and came to Mount Sinai where Moses assembled the whole nation. The top of the mountain was covered with a cloud. It was no ordinary nimbus or cumulus cloud. The Bible says that "the glory of the Lord rested on Mount Sinai, and the cloud covered it for six days; and on the seventh day He called to Moses from the midst of the cloud" (Exodus 24:16). That cloud was the glory of the Lord. The English term "glory" is a translation of the Hebrew *kabod*. It literally means "to be heavy." The glory cloud was heavy with the presence of God. It was a visible manifestation of the divine presence that demanded worship. God was making known the glory of his presence at Sinai in order that his assembled people in turn might glorify him.

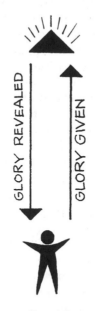

Figure 1:
The Rhythm of Worship

The same glory cloud accompanied the tabernacle as God's people traveled through the desert toward the Promised Land (Exodus 29:43; 33:19–23; 40:34–38). They again saw the cloud when they reached their new home. The glory cloud was revealed on the day Solomon's temple was dedicated on Mount Zion: "The house of the Lord was filled with a cloud, so that the priests could not stand to minister because of the cloud, for the glory of the Lord filled the house of God" (II Chronicles 5:13, 14). No wonder the people responded by bowing in worship and praise (II Chronicles 7:3). God had revealed himself, and worship was the appropriate response to his revelation.

Have you ever observed a visible cloud descend over a place of worship today? Does this mean that God no longer reveals his glory? On the contrary, the glory cloud that appeared in the Old Testament reemerges in the New Testament. The equivalent term for *kabod* is used of Christ in John 1:14(NIV): "The Word became flesh and lived for a while among us. We have seen his *glory*." The glory of divine presence was with Jesus Christ, the coequal Son of God. This was visibly portrayed on the mount of transfiguration where the disciples saw Christ's glory: "A cloud formed and began to overshadow them . . . .And a voice came out of the cloud, saying, 'This is My Son, My Chosen One; listen to Him!'" (Luke 9:34, 35). Today God continues to reveal his glory through the spiritual presence of Jesus Christ, and this is the basis for our response of true worship in which we give glory to the self–revealing God.

Figure 2:
The Glory of God (*Kabod*)

GOD TOOK THE INITIATIVE
TO REVEAL HIS ATTRIBUTES AND ACTS

One's concept of God strongly shapes one's worship. Suppose someone asked you to describe God. Where would you begin? Would you picture a gray-bearded, elderly gentleman perched on a throne? Some people think of God as a cosmic bellhop obligated to meet their every whim. Others consider him to be a resident policeman leaning over the balcony of heaven ready to reprimand those who dare enjoy themselves. Because one's view of God is bound to affect one's worship, it is important to see God as he is and not as we conceive him. Consequently, a growing understanding of God's attributes and acts can be a powerful stimulus to worship.

Consider the magnitude and wonder of God's attributes as revealed in Scripture. The Psalms are especially full of references to these characteristics of God. An understanding of these attributes leads the Psalmist to lift up praise. For example, the familiar Psalm 100 gives an invitation to enter God's courts with thanksgiving and praise. Why? "For the Lord is good; His lovingkindness is everlasting, and His faithfulness to all generations" (v. 5). The divine attributes of goodness, lovingkindness, and faithfulness elicit worship.

Suppose someone handed you a blank piece of paper. Would you be able to list ten or fifteen additional attributes of the triune God? Why not try it right now?

The Bible is a gold mine of information about the character of Almighty God. The infinite, majestic God of the universe was willing to reveal his character to finite humans. He and only he makes it possible for us to know and understand him. But our understanding is not for the purpose of storing cognitive data in our memory bank. God has revealed who he is so that we in turn might obey him and give him the praise of which he is supremely worthy.

God's revelation of himself through his actions in history is also a basis for our worship. The Old Testament is filled with the record of God's great deeds. God's act of redeeming Israel from Egypt motivated Moses to write a hymn of praise (Exodus 15:1–18). Moses wrote another worship song at the end of his life (Deuteronomy 31:30–32:43). It was a praise-filled recital of God's mighty acts with Israel. Likewise Deborah and Barak sang a rehearsal of the righteous acts of the Lord (Judges 5:1–11). The Psalms are replete with recitals of praise to God for his acts of creating and sustaining the world and delivering his people from bondage.

You might find it helpful to try an experiment in your private worship this week. Read a passage of Scripture. Then reread it with paper and pencil in hand. Look for any references to the attributes and acts of the Father, Son or Holy Spirit. What does the passage teach you about who the triune God is and what he has done? Make a list of these attributes and acts. Then use the list to spend time prayerfully praising God. Thank him for who he is and what he has done. This can be a very helpful exercise to expand your view of God and add depth to your experience of worship. Try it!

Scripture Passage: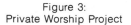

ATTRIBUTES	ACTS

Figure 3:
Private Worship Project

13

Questions for Review

1. What is the foundational principle of worship covered in this chapter?

2. What is the significance of God's name for worship? (Genesis 35:11; 4:26; Exodus 6:2; 20:24; I Kings 11:36; Jeremiah 7:12)

3. Where did the glory cloud appear in the Old Testament and what did it signify? (Exodus 24:16; 29:43; 33:19–23; 40:34–38; II Chronicles 5:13, 14; 7:3)

4. Where do we see the glory cloud in the New Testament? (John 1:14; Luke 9:34, 35)

5. What does knowing God's revealed acts and attributes have to do with worship? (Psalm 100; Exodus 15:1–18; Deuteronomy 31:30–32; Judges 5:1–11)

Questions for Discussion

1. In many churches the focus of the services is on man and his needs instead of God and his glory. Do you agree or disagree with this statement? Explain.

2. What are some ways the name of God is used in the worship service in your church?

3. How should the "rhythm of worship" reflect itself in Sunday services?

4. What are some common misconceptions of God today? What effect do these misconceptions have on worship?

5. What are some examples of acts and attributes of the triune God for which you can give him worship?

---

[1]Robert Webber, "Agenda for the Church: 1976-2000," *Eternity*, (January, 1976, pp. 15, 16).

2

UNCOVERING TREASURE

The Old Testament evidence is presented to demonstrate that worship is an assembly of God's people in his very presence. This chapter also presents the Old Testament evidence for the regulative principle of worship.

Are you the kind of person who is curious and likes to explore unknown territory? Is the Old Testament unknown territory for you? It may be that for you the Old Testament is like a darkened room full of valuable treasures. But faithful study of its thirty-nine books will shed light on those priceless treasures and uncover a wealth of teaching on the subject of worship. You are invited to enter this room and discover two basic principles of worship.

A BASIC ELEMENT OF WORSHIP IN THE OLD TESTAMENT IS THE PRESENCE OF GOD AMONG HIS ASSEMBLED PEOPLE

Most individuals enjoy being with people. Gregarious instincts lead them to meet together for clubs, concerts, political rallies and sports events. The church also is a meeting together of people. The common New Testament word for church, *ecclesia,* is the equivalent of the Old Testament term *qahal*, which means "assembly" or "congregation."

What is it that makes the assembly of the church unique? Why is it different from other types of meetings? The church is different because it is an assembly of God's people *in his very presence.* The assembling of the church is a meeting with God as well as with fellow believers. The assembly is an extraordinary, supernatural event. This is implicit in the very term *church*.

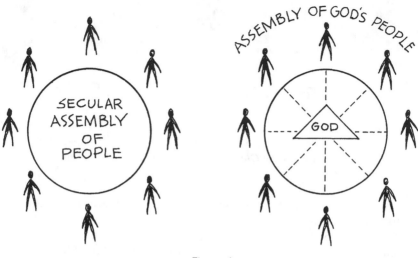

Figure 4:
The Uniqueness of Church Worship Assemblies

God's people assembled for worship regularly during the Old Testament period, and God manifested his presence in those assemblies (at Mount Sinai, in the tabernacle and in the temple on Mount Zion). God declared his presence in those assemblies in several ways.

We have already considered the significance of the divine name as a sign of the divine presence. God said, " ... in every place where I cause My name to be remembered, I will come to you and bless you" (Exodus 20:24). God's name was associated with certain places where he revealed himself (revealed his name) to Israel. These places came to be places for worship because God's name was there. Because God's name was there, Israel understood that God was present there in some special way. Likewise, we have seen the significance of God's glory, the *kabod*, as indicative of the divine presence. At Mount Sinai "the glory of the Lord was like a consuming fire on the mountain top" (Exodus 24:17). This was a visible manifestation that the omnipresent God was present in a special way as his people assembled for worship.

A third manifestation of the divine presence was what the Old Testament describes as "meeting God face to face." When Moses was at Mount Sinai God chose to reveal his face. "The Lord spoke to you face to face at the mountain from the midst of the fire" (Deuteronomy 5:4; cf. Exodus 33:11). Does this mean that we can know what the face of God looks like? No, we are not to confuse the kind of face one sees in the mirror each morning with the face of the infinite God of the universe. He is a spirit without physical parts. To refer to "the face of God" is to use a figure of speech known as an anthropomorphism. The term suggests not a face but rather God's real presence—a presence in which direct personal communication takes place. What else can one do but bow in worship when standing "face to face" with the Almighty God?

Worship, then, can be understood as seeking the face of God and entering into his immediate presence. As the Psalmist writes, "When Thou didst say, 'Seek My face,' my heart said to Thee, 'Thy face, O Lord, I shall seek' " (27:8). This is a mandate for Christians to gather in worship to seek Jehovah's face. Such assemblies for worship often conclude with a familiar benediction that refers to the face of God: "The Lord bless you, and keep you; the Lord make His face shine on you, and be gracious to you; the Lord lift up His countenance on you, and give you peace" (Numbers 6:24–26). Listen for references to the face of God the next time you assemble with God's people for public worship.

One basic principle to be learned from the Old Testament is that *worship implies the presence of God among his assembled people.* (This same principle can also be seen in the New Testament, as will be shown in a later chapter.) What does this principle imply for contemporary Christians? It means that when one enters a service of worship he is entering into the very presence of God. Just as God came to Israel and was present with them in a real way, so also is God present among Christians when they assemble together. His name is upon them, his glory is manifested to them (in Jesus Christ) and he makes his face to shine upon them.

When the alarm goes off on Sunday morning, how easy it is to turn over and ignore it. How easy to rationalize, "I'll sleep in just this one Sunday and catch a church program on TV later." So you attend the "church of the inner spring." How strange it is to forget that corporate worship is an appointment with the living God. A highlight of your week should be assembling for worship in the immediate presence of your Lord.

WORSHIP IS REGULATED BY THE TRIUNE GOD IN HIS WRITTEN REVELATION OF SCRIPTURE

Picture this in your mind. It is a crisp Saturday in October. The football stadium is filled with fans. The two teams come running onto the field. But there are no referees and no captains. All rules of the game are discarded. The result is chaos, as you can well imagine. A football game cannot be played without rules and regulations. The same is true in worship. Man is not free to make up the rules as he goes along. The triune God, who alone is worthy of worship, has instituted the principles under which he is to be given homage. Basing the practice of worship on only what can be derived from Scripture is known as the regulative principle of worship.

TRUE WORSHIP   FALSE WORSHIP

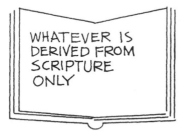

WHATEVER IS DERIVED FROM SCRIPTURE ONLY

WHATEVER IS FORBIDDEN IN SCRIPTURE OR NOT DERIVED FROM SCRIPTURE

Figure 5:
The Regulative Principle of Worship

The Westminster Confession of Faith defines the regulative principle as follows:

18

The acceptable way of worshipping the true God is instituted by Himself, and so limited by His own revealed will, that He may not be worshipped according to the imaginations and devices of men, or the suggestions of Satan, under any visible representation, or any other way not prescribed in the holy Scripture. (XXI:1)

Or it may be more succinctly stated: "Since the Holy Scriptures are the only infallible rule of faith and practice, the principles of public worship must be derived from the Bible, and from no other source."[1]

The regulative principle has ample support in the Old Testament ceremonial law and moral law. Under the ceremonial law God's will for worship was specified in detail. When the tabernacle was constructed God commanded that it be built according to a very specific plan which he revealed in detail (see Exodus 25–27). Elsewhere Jehovah stated, "You shall not add to the word which I am commanding you, nor take away from it . . ." (Deuteronomy 4:2).

There is recorded a sobering story of two priests who disregarded regulative worship by introducing their own ideas. Nadab and Abihu offered strange fire before the Lord which he had not ordered. "And fire came out from the presence of the Lord and consumed them, and they died before the Lord" (Leviticus 10:2). This event confirmed that God required Israel to worship in accordance with his revealed will.

The ceremonial law had minute regulations in connection with tabernacle and temple worship that are no longer binding. Christ came and fulfilled the ceremonial law. However, this does not mean that the regulative principle is now obsolete. There is also a moral law — the Ten Commandments — which specifies God's will concerning worship. This moral law is still operative. The first four commandments in particular must govern our worship today.

The first commandment specifies the object of true worship (Exodus 20:3). True worship must be given to the true God exclusively. No room is allowed for the worship of idols, saints, angels, the virgin Mary, or any other person or object in the universe.

19

On the Saturday night before Easter the Russian Orthodox churches have an evening vigil. As the door to the sanctuary opens you can see a casket being carried. You walk over to the casket and see an image of Jesus Christ lying there. They do not want to violate the second commandment. So the image of Christ is not three-dimensional but a flat cardboard figure. Is this practice in accordance with the regulative principle?

The second commandment specifies that the manner of true worship must be spiritual rather than physical. Worship is not through visual representations (Exodus 20:4-6). The explanation given in the Westminster Shorter Catechism is that "the second commandment requireth the receiving, observing, and keeping pure and entire, all such religious worship and ordinances as God hath appointed in his Word. The second commandment forbiddeth the worshipping of God by images, or any other way not appointed in his Word" (Questions 50, 51). We are not forbidden to create and enjoy representational art. The creative arts are not sinful in themselves. We are forbidden, however, to worship God by means of visual representations. Visuals can be a hindrance to worship by obscuring God's glory. Isaiah's pointed question is, "To whom then will you liken God? Or what likeness will you compare with Him?" (Isaiah 40:18). There can be no answer to that question—only dead silence! The triune God cannot be visibly portrayed without obscuring his glory. Likewise, visuals can lead to erroneous ideas about the triune God. This is what happened when the Israelites at Sinai made a visible symbol of God in the form of a golden calf. They violated the second commandment.

We should recognize the danger of misusing visual representations in our places of worship. We need to ask such questions as this: Can we legitimately include pictures of Christ in our stained glass windows and on murals in our church buildings? What are the practical implications of the second commandment when it requires that true worship be spiritual rather than physical? Just what restrictions does the second commandment impose when it forbids worship through visual representations? It is often a temptation to allow aesthetic and physical stimulation to replace the spiritual reality of true worship.

The third commandment specifies the attitude God desires in our worship (Exodus 20:7). True worship requires a reverent attitude toward the Lord God. The idea of reverence is also conveyed in the most common Old Testament word for worship, *shahah*. It is the equivalent of *proskuneo* in the New Testament and means "to do reverence to, to bow down." Its use is illustrated in II Chronicles 7:3 where it is recorded that "all the sons of Israel, seeing the fire come down and the glory of the Lord upon the house, bowed down on the pavement with their faces to the ground, and they worshiped and gave praise to the Lord . . ." God desires that we recognize his worthiness and bow in his holy presence to hold his name in high regard. Thus some churches encourage worshipers to kneel as part of the liturgy. Whether you physically kneel or not, you should cultivate a heart attitude of reverence when entering the Lord's presence in worship. Churches would do well to study ways to encourage godly reverence in the Sunday worship service. Likewise, parents would do well to instruct their children and to set a good example in this regard.

The fourth commandment specifies one appointed time for worship (Exodus 20:8–11). Certainly all our time is to be used to glorify God. Yet true worship requires setting aside one day out of seven for corporate worship. God has given us freedom as to the hour of the service and its length. But he has prescribed the day. With the resurrection of Christ there was a shift from the seventh day to the first day. Christians may meet for worship any day during the week. Yet they dare not neglect meeting on the first day for this purpose. The Westminster Shorter Catechism explains, "The fourth commandment requireth the keeping holy to God such set times as he hath appointed in his Word; expressly one whole day in seven, to be a holy Sabbath to himself" (Question 58).

There are many changes occurring in American society with respect to the organization of the week. It is more common to find commerce taking place all seven days of the week. Sunday is no longer everyone's day off. It's not that people are working more hours, it's just that different people have different days off from work. In this situation must we continue to hold out for Sunday as the day of Christian worship? Why not have the church gather on Friday night or Saturday morning? Again, we need to ask: What does the regulative principle imply for this question?

The yardstick for evaluating worship services is not tradition or expediency, but rather the written word of the Lord God. True worship includes whatever is derived from Scripture alone.

You might find it stimulating to use the first four commandments in your private worship times this week. Pray through these commandments. Martin Luther did this. He would take each commandment and first reflect on what the Lord requires in it. Next he would look for reasons for thanksgiving in each command. Then he would make it a reason for confession of sin. He would conclude by making it a prayer of petition. Try it!

COMMAND-MENT	WHAT DOES THE LORD REQUIRE?	REASONS FOR THANKSGIVING
1.		
2.		
3.		
4.		

Figure 6:
Prayer Project

Questions for Review

1. What is the first theological principle of worship discussed in this chapter?

2. Explain the significance of the term *church* in relation to worship.

3. Describe three ways God indicated his presence in Old Testament worship assemblies. (Exodus 20:24; 24:15–17; 33:11; Deuteronomy 5:4; Psalm 27:8)

4. What is the regulative principle of worship?

5. What are some examples of Old Testament support for the

ITEMS FOR CONFESSION	ITEMS FOR PETITION

regulative principle of worship? (Exodus 25:40; 20:1–11; Deuteronomy 4:2; Leviticus 10:2)

6. Explain the meaning of the first four commandments of the moral law in relation to worship. (Exodus 20:1–11)

Questions for Discussion

1. Why does the Old Testament have to be consulted for information about the nature and practice of worship? Can't we just skip over it and read what the New Testament has to say?

2. What can be done to impress upon Christians the importance of corporate assembly for worship? Some people think they can worship better privately.

3. What kinds of visual art do you believe can be properly used in church buildings?

4. What are some ways both churches and parents can encourage godly reverence in worship services?

5. What do you think the church should do about sociological and cultural changes that make it increasingly difficult for Christians to assemble on Sundays as the official day of worship?

---

[1]*The Book of Church Order of the Presbyterian Church in America,* Part III, (Decatur, Georgia: Committee for Christian Education and Publications, 1981) 47-1.

3

A GARDEN AND A TENT

This chapter contrasts the immediacy of worship in Eden with the divinely revealed prescriptions for worship associated with the tabernacle. The theological significance of the tabernacle and its liturgy is explained.

A folk song by Joni Mitchell repeats the line, "We've got to get ourselves back to the garden." Myriad attempts have been made down through history to get back to the garden, to return to man's original, idyllic existence. What was so appealing about that garden? That question will be answered in this chapter as the development of worship from the Garden of Eden through the period of the tabernacle is discussed. The time you spend in worship can be far more significant to you as you understand the biblical beginnings of worship.

EARLIEST WORSHIP

God created us in his image with the capacity for divine worship. This distinguishes humans from all other forms of life whether plant or animal. The Bible says: "In the image of God He created him; male and female He created them . . . . Then the Lord God formed man of dust from the ground, and breathed into his nostrils the breath of life; and man became a living soul" (Genesis 1:27; 2:7). This original worship before the fall was not hindered by the barrier of sin. It was natural and immediate. Adam and Eve could experience direct fellowship with their Creator and constantly be in his immediate presence. But that fellowship was ruptured once the fall into sin occurred. Genesis 3:8 states, "And they heard the sound of the Lord God walking in the garden in the cool of the day, and the man and his wife hid themselves from the presence of the Lord God among the trees of the garden." From that day on, worship was not the same. Adam and Eve were expelled from the garden and its immediacy of worship. Thereafter one finds the necessity of altar sacrifices in approaching God. The first chapter after the fall records sacrifices made by Cain and Abel (Genesis 4:3–5). Because there were no priests in this period, the patriarchs fulfilled the priestly role in their families by offering sacrifices. This was true of Noah, Abraham, Isaac, Jacob and Moses who offered altar sacrifices to approach Jehovah in worship. Public worship probably occurred regularly as reflected in the repeated expression "people began to call on the name of the Lord" (Genesis 4:26; 12:8; 13:4; 21:33; 26:25). This was the very simple beginning of corporate worship.

TABERNACLE WORSHIP

Visit a campground on a summer weekend and you can see row upon row of camping trailers and multicolored tents. Camping has become a national pastime. Consequently, a number of Americans have had the experience of pitching a tent. The ancient Israelites also had the experience of pitching a tent—God's tent—called the tabernacle.

The Lord assembled his people at Mount Sinai after he had liberated them from Egypt. Through his spokesman Moses, he issued divine orders which included regulations concerning worship. The people were instructed to construct a special tent that would serve as the place for worship during the wilderness wanderings. It was to be placed in an outer courtyard half the length of a football field. The materials used in construction included "gold, silver and bronze, blue, purple and scarlet material, fine linen, goat hair, rams' skins dyed red, porpoise skins, acacia wood, oil for lighting, spices for the anointing oil and for the fragrant incense, onyx stones and setting stones" (Exodus 25:3–7). The careful artistic details made it an aesthetic delight. Each detail was important because the tabernacle was to be an earthly "copy and shadow of the heavenly things" (Hebrews 8:5).

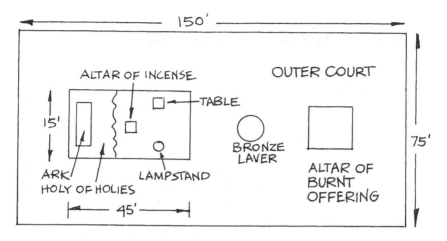

Figure 7:
Floor Plan of the Tabernacle

A. Theological significance of the tabernacle

What was the theological significance of this portable structure? It demonstrated spiritual truths in a visible way. A large veil separated the holy place from the holy of holies. Only the high priest could enter the holy of holies. This priestly mediation as well as the veil served as protection from the wrath of God's holy presence. Both were used in order that God's wrath would not break forth on his stiff-necked people. The immediacy of garden worship was gone. The tabernacle graphically reminded worshipers of this reality in a fallen world.

However, there was a further significance to the tabernacle. It was the place of the divine presence where worship could occur. This reality of divine presence was indicated in several ways.

First, the names used for the tabernacle emphasized God's presence. It was called the "dwelling place" (*Mishkan*) because it was the location where God chose to dwell among his people. "Tent of meeting" (*Ohel-Mo'edh*) was another name. Why? Because God met there with his people as they assembled for worship. Sometimes it was called the "holy place" (*Mikdash*). This reminded the people that the tabernacle was a place set apart by virtue of the localization of God's holy presence.

Second, God stated directly that the purpose of the tabernacle was that he might be with his people. "Let them construct a sanctuary for Me, that I may dwell among them" (Exodus 25:8).

Furthermore, the ark of the covenant was symbolic of the divine presence. It was a small chest overlaid with gold and covered by a mercy seat that especially represented the place where the omnipresent God chose to dwell. The ark suggested the throne of God (Jeremiah 3:16, 17) and the footstool of God (I Chronicles 28:2; Psalm 99:5; 132:7) as symbols of God's perpetual role and presence. Hovering over the mercy seat were two golden cherubim with outstretched wings (I Chronicles 28:18). This designated it as the abode of God (I Chronicles 13:6). Scripture speaks of "the Lord who thrones between the cherubim..." (I Chronicles 13:6; cf. Exodus 25:22).

Figure 8:
The Ark of the Covenant in the Most Holy Place

Fourth, the glory cloud (*kabod*), which was a visible manifestation of the divine presence, filled the tabernacle at its dedication. "Then the cloud covered the tent of meeting, and the glory of the Lord filled the tabernacle. And Moses was not able to enter the tent of meeting because the cloud had settled on it, and the glory of the Lord filled the tabernacle" (Exodus 40:34, 35). The tabernacle was heavy with the localized presence of Jehovah. He had shown

28

his approval of the tabernacle and his desire for people to assemble there in his presence for worship. This same cloud accompanied the tabernacle through all the wilderness wanderings (Exodus 40: 36–38). Worship was centralized in this tent-like structure for several decades.

B. The liturgy of the tabernacle

Suppose you could enter a time capsule and go back to the days of the tabernacle. What would you find in attending a tabernacle worship assembly? You would find something significantly different from what Christians experience in today's worship. The heart of tabernacle worship was the sacrificial system of the ceremonial law. This sacrificial system was founded in the covenant offerings made by Moses at Mount Sinai to atone for the sins of the people (Exodus 24:4–8). God gave detailed instructions on the sacrifices to be made at the tabernacle.

This sacrificial system was not mechanical ritual designed merely to effect subjective changes in the feelings of the worshipers. It was a system designed to provide atonement for sins committed against God. The shed blood of a substitute was offered to expiate the holy wrath of God which was justly on sinners. All these atoning sacrifices prefigured the one perfect atonement that would be made by Christ on the cross. Tabernacle worship anticipated the worship you can experience today.

A common problem in worship services today is restlessness. Many people are bored with sitting passively. The "one-man-show" approach frustrates them. They can't square what is occurring in their church with the biblical doctrine of the priesthood of every believer. They are right in their concern. Christian worshipers are not to be left standing outside in the courtyard as the people in the tabernacle were. The Israelites were not allowed to enter the tabernacle in worship. That was a prerogative reserved for the priests. A special priestly caste had been formed from Aaron and his descendants in the tribe of Levi (Exodus 28, 29). Priests were responsible to represent the people before God in offering sac-

29

rifices for atonement. Their work was "to do the service of the tabernacle of the Lord, and to stand before the congregation to minister to them" (Numbers 16:9). The word "service" in this verse is *leitourgia* in the Greek Old Testament (Septuagint) and is the word from which is derived the English word "liturgy." Liturgy was the work of the priests in the tabernacle.

Things are different now. Jesus Christ came and fulfilled the role as our great High Priest making a perfect once-for-all sacrifice. Thus *all* who are united to Christ are priests and can perform liturgy (I Peter 2:5; Revelation 1:6). God had promised this at the Mount Sinai assembly: "You shall be to Me a kingdom of priests" (Exodus 19:6). This promise has now been fulfilled through Christ. Unlike in tabernacle worship, believers can all participate in entering the holy place to worship the Lord. You are responsible to see that your priesthood is exercised instead of standing outside in the courtyard. Praise God for the privilege of priesthood!

The tabernacle liturgy was placed in the time framework of a calendar instituted by God. The calendar was composed of sabbatical seasons and pilgrimage festivals. These were carefully observed. The sabbatical seasons were as follows:

NAME	TIME	REFERENCE
SABBATH DAY	SEVENTH DAY OF EACH WEEK	GEN 2:3 EX. 20:11; 31:13-17
NEW MOON SABBATH (FEAST OF TRUMPETS)	BEGINNING OF YEAR ON FIRST DAY OF SEVENTH MONTH	LEV. 23:24
DAY OF ATONEMENT	ANNUALLY ON TENTH DAY OF SEVENTH MONTH	LEV. 23:26-32
SABBATICAL YEAR	EVERY SEVENTH YEAR	LEV. 25:1-7
JUBILEE YEAR	EVERY FIFTIETH YEAR	LEV. 25:10

Figure 9:
Sabbatical Seasons of the Ceremonial Law

Three annual pilgrimage festivals were also held. When the Israelites settled in the Promised Land, the pilgrims would gather at Jerusalem for worship and covenant renewal on these festal days.

NAME	TIME	REFERENCE
PASSOVER AND FEAST OF UNLEAVENED BREAD	FOURTEENTH DAY OF FIRST MONTH	EX. 12; 13:3-9; 23:15; LEV.23:5; NUM.28:6-25
FEAST OF WEEKS (HARVEST, OR FIRST-FRUITS, OR PENTECOST)	SEVEN WEEKS AFTER PASSOVER	DEUT. 16:9-12 EX. 23:16
FEAST OF TABERNACLES (BOOTHS OR INGATHERING)	FIVE DAYS AFTER DAY OF ATONEMENT	EX. 23:16 LEV. 23:34

Figure 10:
Pilgrimage Festivals of the Ceremonial Law

The early worship of God's people was shaped by this calendar. But Christians do not continue to observe it today. It was part of the ceremonial law that found fulfillment with Christ (Colossians 2:16). The only worship day still operative is the weekly sabbath day which is a creation ordinance and part of the permanent moral law. The church needs to remain alert to the dangers of imposing a new calendar for worship. Some churches adhere to the church year with celebration of Advent, Epiphany, Lent, Eastertide and Pentecost. This can be valuable in rehearsing the mighty acts of God in Christ on a regular cycle. Christians must be cognizant, however, of the danger of imposing a church year calendar in a legalistic way that regresses to the ceremonial aspects of the old covenant worship. Believers celebrate each Sunday as the fulfillment Christ brought to tabernacle worship. An understanding of that early worship can enrich your appreciation for what you now have in Jesus Christ.

How can you personally apply the doctrine of the priesthood of every believer? You will find a chart below designed to encourage life application. Complete the chart and take the appropriate actions to implement it.

Ways I am now exercising my priesthood in the Sunday worship service of my church	Ways I can improve my participation in corporate worship beginning this Sunday

Figure 11:
My Participation in Corporate Worship

32

Questions for Review

1. Why was worship possible in the Garden of Eden and what distinguished it from later worship? (Genesis 1:27; 2:7; 3:8; 4:3–5)

2. What was the theological significance of the tabernacle? (Hebrews 8:5; Exodus 25:8; 40:34-38)

3. What was the purpose of the sacrificial system of the ceremonial law? (Exodus 24:4–8)

4. Describe the tabernacle system of priesthood and explain how it has been fulfilled today. (Exodus 28, 29; 19:6; Numbers 16:9; I Peter 2:5; Revelation 1:6)

5. What was the time framework used for tabernacle worship assemblies? (Exodus 12; 20:11; 23:15, 16; 31:13–17; Leviticus 23:24–25:10)

Questions for Discussion

1. What are some ways the fall in the Garden of Eden affects corporate worship today? Suppose the fall had not occurred. How would worship differ from what it is today?

2. What are some reasons the Scripture records such minute details concerning the pattern and building of the tabernacle?

3. What do you see in the tabernacle that points ahead to Christ?

4. How do you think Christians should be allowed to exercise their priesthood in the Sunday worship services of the church?

5. Do you think Christians today should or should not observe the traditional church year calendar? What are the advantages and disadvantages?

4

VISITING TEMPLE AND SYNAGOGUE

The theological significance and liturgy of the temple on Mount Zion is discussed as well as the development of the early synagogue and its influence on the worship of the church.

The jumbo jet touches down at Lod Airport in Tel Aviv. Another group of tourists deplane to begin their adventure in Israel. A highlight for most tourists is visiting the ancient city of Jerusalem. They are given the opportunity to see the famous Wailing Wall or Western Wall. It is part of the retaining wall from Herod's temple of the first century. One of the stones uncovered by archaeologists measures sixteen and a half feet long and thirteen feet wide, larger than an automobile. Some of the stones weigh an impressive eighty to one hundred tons each. Jews have come to this wall for centuries to weep over the destruction of the sacred temple. It is a moving experience to visit this place. The Christian tourist can be especially appreciative because the temple has had such a shaping influence on the worship of the Christian church.

TEMPLE WORSHIP

In the last chapter we saw the tabernacle as the focal point of early worship. This terminated after the Israelites settled in the Promised Land. King David wanted to construct a permanent house of worship but was not permitted by God to do so. He did, however, begin preparations by gathering building materials. His son Solomon was responsible for the construction of the first temple on Mount Zion in Jerusalem. The pattern for this temple was similar to the tabernacle except for its larger size and more ornate design. The furnishings had symbolic meaning in portraying spiritual reality to be revealed later in the history of God's people.

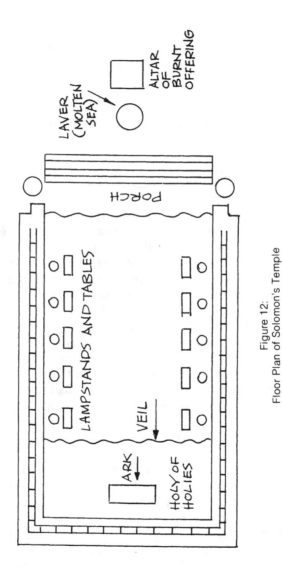

Figure 12:
Floor Plan of Solomon's Temple

This magnificent temple was destroyed in 586 B.C. and its contents were carried to Babylon. When the people returned from captivity a second temple was built under Zerubbabel and completed in 515 B.C. Zerubbabel's temple was similar to the first temple except that it lacked the ark of the covenant which had apparently been destroyed during the Babylonian exile.

Later, King Herod decided to remodel and enlarge the temple. This project began in 20–19 B.C. and continued until A.D. 70, the year the Roman armies of Titus swept down on Jerusalem and destroyed the temple. This was the temple often visited by Christ during his incarnation. On the same spot today one finds the Muslim Dome of the Rock Mosque. It is the large gold-domed temple often seen on television commercials produced by the Israeli Tourist Bureau.

A. Theological significance of the temple

The spiritual significance of the temple was that it was the place where the omnipresent God chose to symbolize his presence for worship. This divine presence was indicated in several ways.

The *kabod* (cloud of glory) filled the temple at its dedication, making all the people acutely aware of God's presence. The Bible states in I Kings 8:10–13 that "when the priests came from the holy place . . .the cloud filled the house of the Lord, so that the priests could not stand to minister because of the cloud, for the glory of the Lord filled the house of the Lord. Then Solomon said, 'The Lord has said that He would dwell in the thick cloud. I have surely built Thee a lofty house, a place for Thy dwelling forever.' " What a moving experience it must have been to be present at the dedication service! The priests and choir were garbed in linen robes. The choir of two hundred and eighty-eight trained musicians was joined by one hundred and twenty trumpeters. Supplementing these was an orchestra with cymbals, lyres and harps. So hundreds of singers and instrumentalists united in musical praise to God. Kenneth Taylor has captured some of the splendor in his *Living Bible* paraphrase of II Chronicles 5:13—"The band and chorus united as one to praise and thank the Lord; their selections were interspersed with trumpet obbligatos, the clashing of cymbals, and the loud playing of other musical instruments—all praising and thanking the Lord. Their theme was 'He is so good! His lovingkindness lasts forever!' '' Can you imagine what it would be like to have a stereophonic recording of that service? God was pleased with this worship given to him and he responded by manifesting the glory of his presence.

Further indications of God's presence in the temple included the ark of the covenant located in the holy of holies. Two golden cherubim with outstretched wings covered the ark showing the reality of the divine presence (I Kings 8:4–7). The name of God also was associated with the temple reminding one of his presence. God placed his name where he chose to dwell. "I have consecrated this house which you have built by putting My name there forever . . ." (I Kings 9:3). Furthermore, the location of the temple was significant. Mount Zion in Jerusalem had been designated as the place of the divine presence. The Psalmist wrote: "Why do you look with envy, O mountains with many peaks, at the mountain which God has desired for His abode? Surely, the Lord will dwell there forever" (68:16). Worshipers could assemble at the temple on Zion with full assurance that God would be in their midst.

Solomon was cognizant of God's localized presence in the temple (I Kings 8:13; II Chronicles 6:2). But he was not naive in his understanding of God. He recognized that Jehovah was not limited to the temple but was the omnipresent Lord of the entire universe. Solomon acknowledged in his dedicatory prayer, "Behold, heaven and the highest heaven cannot contain Thee, how much less this house which I have built!" (I Kings 8:27). Our omnipresent God chose to localize his presence in a special way as his people assembled for worship at the temple.

B. The liturgy of the temple

What kinds of activities would a visitor have found at the temple? The liturgy was strikingly similar to that of the tabernacle. The sacrificial offerings of the ceremonial law were continued. The altar of burnt offerings occupied a prominent place in the outer courtyard where the people assembled. King David had reorganized the Levitical priests in a new system of temple responsibility (I Chronicles 23–26). These priests were overseers of the sacrificial offerings. They participated in daily worship at the temple. The Bible describes their work thus: "They are to stand every morning to thank and to praise the Lord, and likewise at evening, and to offer all burnt offerings to the Lord, on the sabbaths, the new moons and the fixed festivals in the number set by the ordinance concerning them, continually before the Lord" (I Chronicles 23:30, 31). The highlights of temple worship were the three annual festival assemblies of Passover, Weeks and Tabernacles (I Kings 9:25). They were pilgrimage festivals when God's people from diverse geographical locations would converge on Mount Zion in Jerusalem. As they came, some would join in singing the famous Psalms of Ascent (120–134). These were events of the highest significance in the ancient liturgical calendar.

Music was an important part of temple worship. King David instituted a choir and appointed Asaph as its director (I Chronicles 16). At least four thousand instrumentalists and two thousand singers were employed in temple music. Their instruments included cymbals, harps, trumpets, lyres, timbrels, stringed instruments and pipes. The emphasis was on joyful praise to God. Temple worship was rather exuberant. Consider the festal celebration at the dedication of Solomon's temple: The choir and orchestra "were to make themselves heard with one voice to praise and to glorify the Lord" (II Chronicles 5:13).

The words used in temple music consisted largely of the Psalms. Many traces of this liturgical usage are evident in the Psalter. The Psalms were characteristically sung antiphonally by choir and congregation. A beautiful example of a liturgical psalm is the familiar one hundred and fiftieth. It begins and ends with *hallelujah*, the Hebrew for "Praise, you, Jehovah." The word "praise" is found thirteen times and is the dominant note of this Psalm. The invitation is given to join in the joy and delight of lifting up adoration to God. This praise is offered in the earthly sanctuary of the temple as well as in the expanse of heaven (vs. 1). God's acts and attributes form the reason for worship (vs. 2). A call is extended to marshall all instruments possible to join in expression of praise. Wind, string and percussion instruments all unite. Worshipers are called upon to blow the horn, sweep the strings, pluck the harp, beat the drum, play the pipe and clang the cymbals. It has been suggested that as each instrument is named in verses 3–5 it joins in the chorus of praise. So the crescendo builds. By the time you come to verse 6 your heart should be overflowing with exultant praise as you sing, "Let everything that has breath praise the Lord. Praise the Lord!"

How sad that there has been such neglect of psalm singing in the contemporary church. An examination of hymnal indexes reveals that few Psalter selections are included in the most popular hymnals. The church that neglects singing psalms of praise has a truncated worship. Your delight in praising the Lord can be amplified as you join again in singing those songs that filled the ancient temple on Zion. You have a rich heritage in temple worship from which to draw.

Why not use that heritage this week? You might find it helpful to undertake a project: to use the Psalms of Ascent (120–134) in your private or family devotions. Read each psalm carefully. It might be helpful to make use of a commentary on the Psalms to enrich your understanding of each psalm. After study of each, find a metrical arrangement of it set to music and sing it. If you have musical ability on the guitar you might try to write your own musical arrangement with chords.

SYNAGOGUE WORSHIP

The temple of Solomon did not last. Although it was an impressive structure, it was destined for destruction. The armies of Babylon swept down on Jerusalem in 586 B.C. They destroyed the temple and took the Jews captive to Babylon. For seventy years God's people were in a foreign land removed from their place of worship. They longed for corporate worship, especially on festival days and sabbaths. So they began to gather in small groups in homes. This marked the beginning of synagogues. The transition was being made from temple to synagogue worship.

Finally the seventy-year captivity was complete. When the Jews returned to Israel they began to construct simple synagogue buildings. The name "synagogue" in Greek is a compound of "together" and "to bring." The people assembled together in these buildings which became the center of religious life in Judaism. Archaeologists have uncovered some of these early synagogues. The furnishings were very simple. An open room contained a chest with rolls of Scripture; a platform with reading desk, lamps, candelabra, trombones and trumpets; and benches for worshipers.

What activities occurred in synagogue worship? This is an important question to answer because synagogue worship has had a stronger shaping influence on the present worship of the church than that of temple worship. An understanding of synagogue worship can heighten our appreciation for contemporary corporate worship.

Figure 13:
The Influence of Our Heritage

Christ regularly attended synagogue services. One sabbath in Nazareth he entered the synagogue "as was His custom" (Luke 4:16). An examination of that service reveals the centrality given to the reading and exposition of Scripture in synagogue worship. This was physically evident because the main article of furniture was a small chest containing scrolls of the Old Testament. It was similar to the ark of the covenant in the tabernacle and the temple containing the stone tablets of God's law. The synagogue chest reminded people of the importance of God's word.

The high value placed on Scripture was also evident in the use of seven readings from the Old Testament in the worship services. A special reading was also given from the Old Testament prophets. Christ as a visiting rabbi was asked to read from the prophet Isaiah.

The appointment of a *chazzan* —mentioned in Luke 4:20—also revealed the high value placed on Scripture. The *chazzan* was a man appointed to care for the sacred rolls of Scripture. He would take them out for the readings and see that they were replaced afterwards.

The high value placed on Scripture was further evident in the way it was read. The reader always stood for this part of the service. Christ stood to read the word at the synagogue in Nazareth (Luke 4:16). Then, each sabbath they would have an exposition of Scripture following its reading. After Christ read the Scripture in Nazareth, he sat down on the platform and began to give an exposition of the passage. The reading and exposition of Scripture was essential to synagogue worship. Indeed, the service of the word was the basic function of the synagogue.

The same emphasis should be true today. Scripture should be conspicuously present in church services. The word of God should be read and preached in each service of worship. The young pastor Timothy was given an apostolic command: "Give attention to the public reading of Scripture, to exhortation and teaching" (I Timothy 4:13). The reason for scriptural readings and expositions in services of worship is not to serve as a time-filler, but to firmly establish the church in her faith. Scripture is read and preached in order that God's people be nurtured and edified. God speaks to us through his living word and we in turn respond by offering our worship up to him.

Imagine what would happen if all Bibles were taken away from the Christian church and an electronic memory eraser then removed all traces of Scripture from the minds of God's people. Can you imagine what Sunday worship services would be like under those conditions? Remove the word of God and you have removed the heart and life of the service. May this never happen. The

42

authoritative, written word should be conspicuously present in worship services. Is the reading and exposition of a balanced diet of Scripture an essential ingredient in the worship of your church?

Questions for Review

1. Identify the various temples that have been built on Mount Zion in Jerusalem.

2. What was the theological significance of the temple? (I Kings 8; II Chronicles 5–6:2; I Kings 9:3; Psalm 68:16)

3. What constituted the liturgy of the temple? (I Chronicles 16; 23–26; II Chronicles 5:13; I Kings 9:25; Psalm 150)

4. How did synagogue worship originate?

5. What can be learned from Christ's visit to the synagogue in Nazareth? (Luke 4:14–30)

Questions for Discussion

1. Was it right for Solomon's temple to be constructed with such elegant splendor? (II Chronicles 3, 4). What does this imply for church building committees today?

2. Should contemporary Christians attempt to recapture the note of joyful praise evident in Old Testament temple worship? Why or why not?

3. How can psalm singing be used in today's worship?

4. Has the church been more influenced by temple worship or by synagogue worship? How?

5. How can corporate worship services reflect the high value placed on Scripture as God's word?

2

Worship Under the
New Covenant

5

FULFILLMENT

This chapter is a presentation of the biblical evidence that points to Jesus Christ as the fulfillment of all the Old Testament forms and ceremonies of worship including the tabernacle, temple, and ceremonial sacrifices. Thus worship should be Christo-centric with the dominant motif being the presence of Christ among his assembled people.

Do you remember the excitement you felt as a child when Christmas approached? Presents, a colorfully decorated tree, and stockings by the fireplace were all part of the excitement of the holiday. As the years pass your appreciation expands beyond the surface festivities to the spiritual reality commemorated at Christmas. What an empty celebration it would be without the incarnation of Christ! This miracle of divine incarnation changed the world. The advent of Christ also dramatically changed worship. The shift from the old phase of the covenant to the new brought about an altered approach to worship. In this chapter you will see how the advent changed and fulfilled the meaning of worship. It is this worship under the new covenant in which you and I and all who call themselves Christian now are called to participate.

CHRIST IS THE FULFILLMENT
OF OLD TESTAMENT WORSHIP

Jesus Christ is the fulfillment of all the Old Testament forms and ceremonies of worship. They were shadows that pointed ahead to Christ. But they were incomplete and only found fulfillment with Christ's coming to dwell with his people. In Christ the meaning and

47

practice of worship was made clear.

A. Fulfillment of the tabernacle

If you had lived during the days of Moses, you would have worshiped at the tabernacle. This tent-like sanctuary accompanied God's people in their wilderness wanderings. Contemporary Christians no longer need to worship at the tabernacle because Jesus Christ fulfilled it — the worship of the tabernacle was but a picture of what Christ came to do. The pre-existent second person of the Godhead came to earth in human form. The Gospel of John describes this incarnation: "The Word became flesh and lived for a while among us" (1:14 NIV). The Greek verb for 'live' (*skenow*) is used in the Greek Old Testament (Septuagint) in the noun form for the 'tabernacle'. It can be translated 'tabernacled'. Christians no longer need to erect the tabernacle because Christ has come to tabernacle among us. Whereas the tabernacle was a sign of God's presence with his people before the time of Christ, now that Christ has come the sign is no longer necessary. God has come in the flesh to dwell with his church.

B. Fulfillment of the temple

Likewise, God's people need not erect another temple on Mount Zion. The body of Christ became the new temple eliminating the need for a physical temple of stones. Jesus explained this one day as he addressed the Jews in the Jerusalem temple. He had driven the money changers and animal merchants from the temple area. This precipitated a demand, " 'What sign do You show to us, seeing that You do these things?' Jesus answered . . . them, 'Destroy this temple, and in three days I will raise it up ' " (John 2:18, 19). The Jews, taking the statement as a literal reference to Herod's temple, were incredulous. Construction had begun on that temple in 20 B.C. and continued for forty-six years. It still was incomplete. So who did he think he was to claim the ability to destroy and rebuild that massive structure in three days? John adds a footnote to explain Christ's statement: "But He was speaking of the temple of His body" (John 2:21). Christ was using a veiled figure of speech that showed his incarnate body on earth was the new temple of God. He had come to fulfill the temple.

What happened when the incarnate body of Christ ascended from planet earth? There was still no need to revive the physical temple. Because those joined to the crucified and resurrected Christ became the Body of Christ, the church. "We are the temple of the living God" (II Corinthians 6:16). Paul describes the new temple of the church in terms of Christ, "In whom the whole building, being fitted together is growing into a holy temple in the Lord; in whom you also are being built together into a dwelling of God in the Spirit" (Ephesians 2:21, 22).

The temple in Jerusalem had long been a focal point for worship. But when Christ came he taught that the focal point would change. He told the Samaritan woman at the well, "Woman, believe Me, an hour is coming when neither in this mountain, nor in Jerusalem, shall you worship the Father" (John 4:21). The hour of Christ's death and resurrection marked a transfer from the temple as *the* place for worship. God's people no longer need an earthly temple on Mount Zion in Jerusalem. They can come through Jesus to the heavenly Jerusalem in joyful assembly (Hebrews 12:18–24). Nor is there ever a need to restore an earthly temple on Mount Zion. Even in heaven, John said, "I saw no temple in [the city], for the Lord God, the Almighty, and the Lamb, are its temple" (Revelation 21:22). Christ has brought fulfillment.

> To restore the temple would be to offer new reason for confidence in the flesh, to build again the wall of partition and to destroy the unity of the people of God. No man can lay another foundation: Jesus Christ is the true, the final, the real temple. He is the glory of Israel, and to him must be the gathering of the nations be.[1]

This theological truth has a practical implication for present worship. Christian worship should not be building-centered. How futile it is to identify buildings with true worship. To become building-centered is to revert to an inferior, old covenant kind of worship. Christians are given freedom to worship in many different styles and forms of building. Climatological and sociological setting can determine the style of building. Some Christians live in nations where it is not possible to erect their own building for corporate worship. But these believers can still exhibit the classical marks of the church: proper preaching of the word, proper administration of the sacraments, and proper exercise of church discipline. Even without a "church" building they can experience the presence of the living Christ who promised "where two or three have gathered together in My name, there I am in their midst" (Matthew 18:20). A church should be bound together by more than a building. The true temple is not made with bricks and stone and lumber. It's made of people united to Jesus Christ who assemble for worship on the Lord's day.

C.   Fulfillment of the sacrifices of the Old Testament ceremonial law

Christ did enter the Jerusalem temple on the festival days of Passover (John 2:15ff.), Tabernacles (John 7:2ff.) and Dedication (John 10:22ff.). But there is no evidence that he ever offered ceremonial sacrifices in the temple. This was unnecessary because he was the fulfillment of them. Christ himself was the spotless Lamb of God, the Passover lamb which was sacrificed (I Corinthians 5:7). He was our High Priest who entered the most holy place to make a once-for-all sacrifice with his own blood for the sins of his people (Hebrews 9:11–10:18).

The crucifixion is the very embodiment of the fulfillment which Christ brought to all the ceremonial law. Imagine that you are sitting on a hill outside the walls of Jerusalem. In the distance you see the silhouettes of three men hanging on wooden crosses. The sky becomes progressively darker. The ground beneath you begins to rumble. You know it's the beginning of an earthquake so you hasten to escape through the narrow streets of the city. Coming toward you are some of the temple priests, excitedly crying, "It's ripped, it's ripped in two!" The massive temple curtain dividing the holy place from the most holy place has been torn by an invisible force. The Bible states, "The veil of the temple was torn in two from top to bottom" (Matthew 27:51). All three synoptic Gospels record this dramatic event. The historians Tacitus and Josephus, as well as the Talmud, refer to it. That massive sixty-by-thirty foot curtain, as thick as the palm of a man's hand, had been supernaturally torn by God the Father. He synchronized it to occur simultaneously with the death of Christ. This event demonstrated that the entire Old Testament ceremonial system of priests and sacrifices had been fulfilled by Jesus Christ. "Therefore, brethren, we have confidence to enter the holy place by the blood of Jesus, by a new and living way which He inaugurated for us through the veil, that is, His flesh" (Hebrews 10:19, 20).

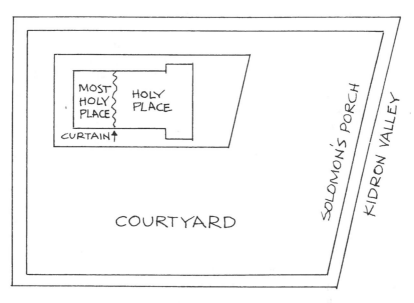

Figure 14:
The Curtain in Herod's Temple

Christ our High Priest has now made all Christians part of the new spiritual priesthood able to enter the most holy place and offer spiritual sacrifices acceptable to God through Christ (I Peter 2:5). New sacrifices have replaced those of the old ceremonial law. What kinds of new sacrifices does God expect of his priests? He desires the sacrifice of self. You are urged "to present your bodies a living and holy sacrifice, acceptable to God, which is your spiritual service of worship" (Romans 12:1). He desires the sacrifice of monetary gifts which are "a fragrant aroma, an acceptable sacrifice, well pleasing to God" (Philippians 4:18). Sacrifices of praise please the Lord. "Through [Jesus] then let us continually offer up a sacrifice of praise to God, that is, the fruit of lips that give thanks to His name" (Hebrews 13:15). Likewise we are reminded, "Do not neglect doing good and sharing; for with such sacrifices God is pleased" (Hebrews 13:16).

Jesus Christ is the fulfiller of all the Old Testament forms and ceremonies of worship. How does this affect present-day worship? It means that the nature of worship is to be Christ-centered. The liturgy of church services should point to Christ and reflect the fulfillment he brought. Several New Testament hymns celebrate Christ's nature and work (Philippians 2:6–11; Colossians 1:15–20; I Timothy 3:16). Prayers are now offered in Christ's name (John 15:16; Ephesians 5:20; Hebrews 13:15). Confessions of faith acknowledge Christ's Lordship (Philippians 2:11; Romans 10:9; I Corinthians 12:3). Baptism is performed in Christ's name (Acts 2:38; 22:16) and signifies union with the crucified and resurrected Christ (Galatians 3:27, 28; Romans 6:2–6) ; Colossians 2:12). The Lord's Supper is centered on the death and promised return of the resurrected Christ (I Corinthians 11:26–29). Even the weekly day on which we meet for worship points to Christ. The Lord's day reminds us of Christ who was resurrected on the first day of the week (Matthew 28:1; Acts 20:7; I Corinthians 16:2; Revelation 1:10). So the nature of New Testament worship is Christ-centered. The hymns, prayers, confessions of faith, sacraments, and Scripture readings all point to Christ the fulfiller of worship. Is this true in your church?

WORSHIP HAS AS ITS DOMINANT MOTIF
THE PRESENCE OF CHRIST
AMONG HIS ASSEMBLED PEOPLE

Christians are commanded to assemble together, "not forsaking our own assembling together, as is the habit of some, but encouraging one another . . ." (Hebrews 10:25). The context shows that this is referring to the corporate worship assembly. It takes place as believers draw near to God unto the most holy place by the blood of Jesus (Hebrews 10:19–22). So Christ is present in our assemblies as he promised. "Where two or three have gathered together in My name, there I am in their midst'' (Matthew 18:20). Although he is not physically present (Mark 14:7), he is present in a special way in the worship assemblies of his saints. So private "worship" on a golf course or lake, or in front of a radio or television set, can never be a satisfactory substitute for corporate assembly. The reality of Christ's spiritual presence gives a special dimension to corporate worship. It is the highlight of the week for the Christian.

Worship has as its dominant motif the presence of Christ among his assembled people. Several practical implications follow. Worship services should be arranged so as to cause Christians to be aware of Christ's presence with them. This awareness is not simply a subjective emotional feeling. The reality of Christ's presence is rooted in the promise of our faithful Lord. The service of worship can be arranged so as to lead worshipers to an awareness of this promised divine presence.

Worship services should also be evangelistic in the sense that Christ's presence is noticeable to an unbeliever entering a service. The New Testament refers to a non-Christian entering a Christian assembly with the result that "he will fall down and worship God, exclaiming, 'God is really among you!' " (I Corinthians 14:25 NIV). Could a non-Christian entering the Sunday morning worship service of your church come to this conclusion? You might use this as a suggestion for daily prayer this week. Pray that believers and non-believers might be aware of the divine presence of Christ in the Sunday morning worship assembly of your church. You might not only add this to your daily prayer list but make it a special matter for prayer in the minutes of silent preparation before Sunday's service. How thankful Christians can be for the reality of the divine presence in corporate worship assemblies! "Let us come before His presence with thanksgiving" (Psalm 95:2). May this truth also move us to increased anticipation for the divine appointment that occurs each Lord's day!

Questions for Review

1. How did Christ fulfill the Old Testament tabernacle? (John 1:14)

2. Explain how Christ is the fulfillment of the Old Testament temple on Mount Zion. (John 2:18–21; Ephesians 2:21, 22; II Corinthians 6:16; John 4:21; Revelation 21:22)

3. What evidence can you give that Christ fulfilled the Old Testament sacrifices of the ceremonial law? (Matthew 27:51; I Corinthians 5:7; Hebrews 9:11–10:20)

4. What are some of the new spiritual sacrifices God expects of you as a priest? (Romans 12:6; Philippians 4:18; Hebrews 13:15, 16)

5. Name some ways in which the nature of New Testament worship is Christ-centered. (Philippians 2:6–11; Colossians 1:15–20; John 15:16; Hebrews 13:15; Romans 10:9; Acts 2:38; Romans 6:2–6; I Corinthians 11:26–29)

6. What are the reasons for saying that worship has as its dominant motif the presence of Christ among his assembled people? (Hebrews 10:18–25; Matthew 18:20; I Corinthians 14:25)

Questions for Discussion

1. It is not necessary to restore an earthly temple on Mount Zion. Do you agree or disagree?

2. What are the advantages and disadvantages of a church owning its own physical building where it meets for worship?

3. What are some examples of ways church services can reflect the fulfillment Christ has brought to worship?

4. What suggestions do you have about how to lead worshipers in your church to an awareness of Christ's presence in services?

5. Corporate worship on the Lord's day should never be replaced by weeknight fellowship groups or by private worship. Do you agree or disagree?

[1] Edmund P. Clowney, "The Final Temple," *The Westminster Theological Journal,* XXV, pp. 156–189.

6

A TASTE OF HEAVEN

Scripture teaches that the angels were present in Old Testament worship assemblies and continue to be present in today's assemblies. Furthermore, there is a heaven/earth link in worship services as believers by faith enter the heavenly Jerusalem in preparation for the future consummated worship of heaven.

What are angels like? Many people dismiss angels as a superstitious product of a pre-scientific imagination. They place angels on the same level as the fairy godmother, the Easter bunny and Santa's elves. Yet the Bible teaches that God has created a vast company of angelic beings. They number "myriads of myriads, and thousands of thousands" (Revelation 5:11). They are creatures who have been created to serve and worship God. They are invisible to the human eye though they have been manifested in visible form on certain occasions. Did you know that these angels have a special relation to the public worship services in your church?

WORSHIP IS THE ASSEMBLY
OF GOD'S EARTHLY PEOPLE
WITH THE ANGELS PRESENT

Angels had a special role in the worship assemblies of God's people in the Old Testament. After the exodus Moses assembled the Israelites at the base of Mount Sinai. Deuteronomy 33:2 describes how "the Lord came from Sinai, and dawned on them from Seir; He shone forth from Mount Paran, and He came from the midst of ten thousand holy ones; at His right hand there was flashing lightning for them." "Ten thousand holy ones" refers to the angelic company. The earthly holy ones, the Israelites, met with the angelic, heavenly holy ones in the presence of God.

The angels were also present at the tabernacle in the wilderness. They were symbolically represented in the two golden cherubim that hovered over the ark of the covenant (Exodus 25:18–22; I Chronicles 13:6; 28:18). The presence of angels was also symbolically represented in the embroidery of cherubim designs on the curtains. God ordered that the tabernacle contain "ten curtains of fine twisted linen and blue and purple and scarlet material . . . with cherubim, the work of a skillful workman" (Exodus 26:1).

The temple on Mount Zion also demonstrated the presence of angels. "The chariots of God are twice ten thousand, thousands upon thousands; the Lord came from Sinai into the sanctuary" (Psalm 68:17). The vast host of angels that had been present at Sinai and at the tabernacle were now present in the holy place of the temple on Mount Zion. They were again symbolically represented in the two golden cherubim as well as the embroidery of cherubim designs on the temple curtains (II Chronicles 3:10–14).

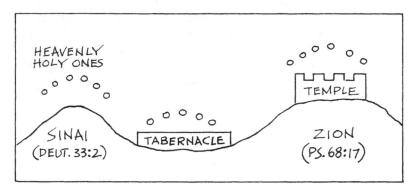

Figure 15:
Angels in Old Testament Assemblies

Did the presence of angels in worship cease with the old covenant? The evidence speaks to the contrary. Angels were prominent in the earthly ministry of Christ. They were present at his birth, temptation in the wilderness, suffering in Gethsemane, resurrection and ascension. They continue to be present with Christians as they assemble in the name of Christ for worship. By faith you now are able to enter the heavenly Jerusalem when you worship. You come through Christ and are promised that you have come to thousands upon thousands of angels in joyful assembly (see Hebrews 12:18–24). The apostle Paul was cognizant of the angelic presence in worship. Thus he encouraged the Corinthian women to wear veils in public worship "because of the angels" (I Corinthians 11:10).

Although angels are present in worship assemblies they are not to receive worship themselves. The Colossians were warned, "Do not let anyone who delights in false humility and the worship of angels disqualify you for the prize" (2:18 NIV). Similarly the apostle John was warned when he fell at the feet of an angel in worship. "Do not do that; I am a fellow-servant of yours and your brethren who hold the testimony of Jesus; worship God!" (Revelation 19:10).

Worship is the assembly of God's earthly people with the angels present. This theological principle has some practical implication for the services in your church. It means there is more happening in the worship service than meets the eye. Worship is a supernatural event. As you assemble to lift up praise to God, you are joined by the invisible angelic hosts. Worship is truly a supernatural happening. It is a heavenly event.

This theological principle also explains why prayers in a worship service often refer to angels. You might hear the minister pray, "We praise you, joining our voices with angels and archangels and with all the company of heaven." Likewise, a number of hymns refer to angels. Learn to listen for this. As you sing hymns that refer to the angelic hosts let it remind you of their presence in your assembly.

> Angels, help us to adore him;
> Ye behold him face to face;
> Sun and moon, bow down before him,
> Dwellers all in time and space,

Praise him, praise him,
Praise him, praise him,
Praise with us the God of grace.

EARTHLY WORSHIP IS DIRECTLY LINKED IN THE PAST AND PRESENT TO THE FUTURE CONSUMMATED WORSHIP OF HEAVEN

"I think I'd be bored to death in that place!" That's the comment of a person not too excited about the prospect of an eternity in heaven. He has an image of his floating around on Posturpedic clouds, wearing a white robe, strumming a golden harp and having a silly halo hanging over his head. Praise God that's not what it's going to be like! God has realities planned that far exceed our present expectations and capacities for understanding. But he has made provision for us to experience a foretaste of heaven in the present. Understanding this can add a new dimension of appreciation to your present worship experiences.

A. Past worship under the old covenant was a shadow of heavenly worship.

We have already seen the link between the heavenly angels and earthly worship at Sinai, the tabernacle and Zion. This uniting of heavenly and earthly worship was vividly portrayed in the dream of Jacob. "He had a dream, and behold, a ladder was set on the earth with its top reaching to heaven; and behold, the angels of God were ascending and descending on it. And behold, the Lord stood above it" (Genesis 28:12, 13). Jacob's ladder visually portrays the invisible link that joined earthly and heavenly worship under the old covenant.

When worshipers came to the tabernacle they were reminded of the link. The tabernacle was "a copy and shadow of the heavenly things" (Hebrews 8:5) and the sacrificial system included "copies of the heavenly things" (Hebrews 9:23). The later temple on Mount Zion contained artistic details that gave a foretaste of heaven. The palm trees and cherubim constituted a reminder of paradise. Past worship under the old covenant was a shadow of heavenly worship.

B. Present worship under the new covenant is a fulfilled participation in heavenly worship through Christ by faith.

The Jacob's ladder of the Old Testament has been fulfilled
through the coming of Jesus Christ. Jesus told Nathanael, "Truly,
truly, I say to you, you shall see the heavens opened, and the
angels of God ascending and descending upon the Son of Man"
(John 1:51). Christ is the link between heaven and earth. He is the
Jacob's ladder by whom we enter heaven every time we worship.

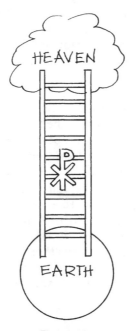

Figure 16:
Jesus Is the Jacob's Ladder

Our crucified and resurrected High Priest has ascended and
"taken His seat at the right hand of the throne of the Majesty in the
heavens" (Hebrews 8:1). He entered "into heaven itself, now to
appear in the presence of God for us" (Hebrews 9:24). Christ's

work means the barricades between heaven and earth are now torn down. Christians may now participate by faith in heavenly worship. God "raised us up with [Christ], and seated us with Him in the heavenly places, in Christ Jesus" (Ephesians 2:6). The union of the earthly church militant with the heavenly church triumphant is a present, though imperfect, reality.

A careful reading of Hebrews 12:18–24 can clarify this truth. Believers are *now* able to approach the heavenly Jerusalem in joyful assembly through Jesus the Mediator of the new covenant. This reality gives meaning to the present earthly assemblies in which Christians worship. Every time we assemble for worship we enter heaven, not physically, but by faith. We do not have to wait until death or the second coming to have a taste of heaven. By faith we are able to enter that dimension now. We can participate in the ceaseless worship that now surrounds the heavenly throne of God. What a cause for rejoicing!

This theological truth can be reflected in the services of your church. Each time you celebrate the Lord's Supper you can do so in anticipation of the marriage supper of the Lamb that will be held in the heavenly dimension (I Corinthians 11:26; Matthew 26:29; Revelation 19:9). Each time you hear the Maranatha prayer, "Come, O Lord," you can be reminded of the entrance of the saints into the heavenlies. The present entrance is in faith but it will be consummated at the return of Christ (I Corinthians 16:22; Revelation 22:20). Each time you sing hymns of praise you can participate in the heavenly chorus that surrounds the throne. The singing of laudatory hymns testifies that the church is even now a participant in the heavenly realities. In the familiar doxology the church sings:

> Praise God from whom all blessings flow;
> Praise Him, all creatures here *below*;
> Praise Him *above*, ye heavenly host;
> Praise Father, Son, and Holy Ghost.

C. Future heavenly worship will be an eternal consummation of the purpose for which man was created.

Christians have been promised the future return of Christ. This advent will be a final assembly of the elect. II Thessalonians 2:1 describes this gathering together by the word *episunagoges*. The cognate verb is used in Matthew 24:31 where we read that Christ "will send forth His angels with a great trumpet, and they will *gather together* His elect from the four winds, from one end of the sky to the other." The noun form of this word is used to describe present earthly worship assemblies in Hebrews 10:25— "our own assembling together." Present worship assemblies can prepare us for the final consummated assembly of the future.

What will the consummated worship of heaven be like? A beautiful description of heavenly worship is given in Revelation 5. We see a scene of Lamb-centered worship. The Lamb, Jesus Christ, is the focal point because he is worthy to open the scroll as the omnipotent and omniscient one. He is worthy because he is co-equal with the Father and was slain to redeem his people. We also see that heavenly worship includes songs of praise. These songs are characterized as being new. Perhaps they will be special songs composed just for heaven. Or this may indicate there will be a sense of freshness to the songs of heaven. They are not going to be golden oldies from ancient hymnals that bore you to death. They will be fresh new songs of praise which should excite you in anticipation.

Not only will the songs be new, they will be God-centered rather than man-centered. A sample song is "Worthy is the Lamb that was slain to receive power and riches and wisdom and might and honor and glory and blessing" (Revelation 5:12). It's a sevenfold ascription of praise that piles word upon word in adoration of Christ. Another example, given in verse 13, is "To Him who sits on the throne, and to the Lamb, be blessing and honor and glory and dominion, forever and ever." It's a fourfold ascription of praise to God the Father and God the Son. Our worship here on earth, therefore, should prepare us for heavenly worship by teaching us to appreciate God-centered songs of praise that focus on the attributes and acts of the triune God.

You can further discover from Revelation 5 that the songs are progressive. The singing begins with the twenty-four elders in a first circle around the throne. These elders are joined by an angelic choir in a second circle around the throne. It's a choir to end all choirs. It numbers ten thousand times ten thousand, and thousands and thousands of angels. You can't take a pocket calculator and figure out the exact number from these figures. The point is that the angelic choir is a vast innumerable host of voices singing to the Lord. Can you imagine what that will sound like?

But that's not all. A third group of voices joins in: "Then I heard every creature in heaven and on earth and under the earth and on the sea, and all that is in them, singing: 'To him who sits on the throne and to the Lamb be praise and honor and glory and power, for ever and ever!' ''(Revelation 5:13 NIV). Perhaps the composer George Frederick Handel has come closer than any other to capturing the sound of that music in his famous oratorio, the *Messiah*. Handel concludes that work with a magnificent piece based on Revelation 5 and entitled "Worthy Is the Lamb." The story is told that after Handel had completed the *Messiah*, his servant discovered the great composer in tears. Handel explained, "I did think that I did see all heaven before me, and the great God himself!"

Did anybody say he thought heaven would be boring? It is not possible! It will be an exciting time of worship and praise uniting the hosts of heaven with all true believers from every tribe, language, people and nation. It will be the ultimate consummated assembly in the immediate presence of the King of kings and Lord of lords.

The principle that has been explained is that *earthly worship is directly linked in the past and present to the future consummated worship of heaven*. This truth has practical implications for your worship. Knowing the present heavenly realities of worship should motivate you to place a high priority on attending weekly worship assemblies. These present gatherings can help prepare you for the future heavenly assembly. God has created his people so that they might glorify him and enjoy him forever.

Knowing of the present heavenly realities should motivate you to reflect heavenly joy in the services in your church. Worship should not be a boring drag. The supernatural realities of joining the heavenly hosts by faith should be evident in the joy of your services.

Knowing of the link between heaven and earth in worship should keep you alert to notice references to this in Scripture readings, prayers and hymns used in your church. You might find it helpful to undertake a project. Take the hymnal used in your church. Flip through the pages and see how many worship hymns refer to the union of heaven and earth in worship. You may find that this experience helps you to be aware and appreciative of the heavenly reality you can now experience in worship services.

Page	Title	Notations

Figure 17:
Personal Study of Hymnic References to the Heaven/Earth Link

Questions for Review

1. What were the main Old Testament worship assemblies where angels were present? (Deuteronomy 33:2; Exodus 25:18–22; I Chronicles 13:6; 28:18; Psalm 68:17; II Chronicles 3:10–14)

2. What reasons do we have for saying that angels are present in worship assemblies today? (Hebrews 12:18–24; I Corinthians 11:10)

3. Give examples of the link that existed between Old Testament earthly worship and heavenly worship. (Genesis 28:10–17; Hebrews 8:5; 9:23)

4. What does it mean to say that Jesus is *the* Jacob's ladder? (John 1:51; Genesis 28:10–17)

5. Explain how believers today can participate in heavenly worship. (Hebrews 8:1; 9:24; 12:18–24; Ephesians 2:6)

6. Describe what the consummated worship of heaven will be like. (Revelation 5; 19:1–9; 21:1–22)

Questions for Discussion

1. What practical implications can be drawn from the principle that angels are present in today's worship assemblies?

2. How can present worship on earth prepare us for heavenly worship?

3. What does the content of heavenly worship have to say to us concerning our present worship? (Revelation 5; 19:1–9; 21:1–22)

4. What are examples of ways the heaven/earth link is being reflected in the worship services of your church?

5. Why are so many hymns in today's hymnals man-centered rather than God-centered? Give examples of both types.

7

REGULATED FREEDOM

New Testament worship is regulated by Christ who has revealed its proper content and has given Scripture so that all "parts" of worship must have explicit or implicit biblical warrant. This chapter concludes with a discussion of the practical implementation of the regulative principle of worship.

The elders of the church are confronted with a decision. One of their church members has requested permission to participate in the Sunday morning worship service. She is a professional choreographer who would like to use her talent to the glory of God. She has created an interpretive dance for the Lord's Prayer and is asking permission to present this artistic expression as an act of worship next Sunday morning. What would you say to her if you were faced with this decision? What should determine whether something is acceptable or not for corporate worship?

The regulative principle of worship can help in making this kind of decision. According to the regulative principle, God alone has the right to regulate the worship offered to him. True worship may include only those elements that are derived from Scripture. Whatever is forbidden in Scripture or not specifically derived from Scripture constitutes a corruption of true worship and makes it unacceptable to God. The Westminster Confession of Faith defines the regulative principle as follows:

> The acceptable way of worshipping the true God is instituted by Himself, and so limited by His own revealed will, that He may not be worshipped according to the imaginations and devices of men, or the suggestions of Satan, under any visible representation, or any other way not prescribed in the Holy Scripture. (XXI:1)

65

The Old Testament support for the regulative principle has already been given in chapter two. "The first covenant had regulations of divine worship . . . ." (Hebrews 9:1). But these regulations of the ceremonial law have been fulfilled in Christ and are no longer to be considered the rule for the church's worship. Yet the worship of the church is still under divine regulation. *New Testament worship is regulated by Christ and we have his instruction in Scripture.*

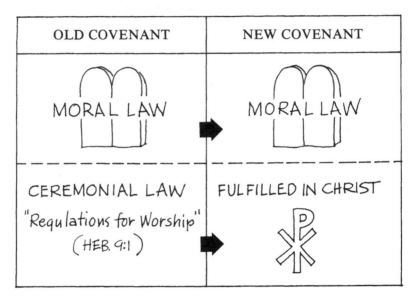

Figure 18:
Transition from Old to New

CHRIST AS THE HEAD
OF THE CHURCH
DIRECTS THE WORSHIP OF HIS PEOPLE

Suppose you asked a cross section of church-goers this question: "Who is in charge of the Sunday morning worship service in your church?" You might hear these answers: "The minister, the worship committee, the elders, the deacons, the music director." Ultimately, however, the one directing worship in the church should be Jesus Christ, our great High Priest and rightful Head of the church. How does Christ as Head direct the worship of his people?

A. Christ directs worship by revealing its proper content.

When one reads through the Gospels he finds a number of instances where Christ participated in public worship. By his own practice in worship, Christ left a pattern for succeeding generations of Christians. For example, Christ taught the pattern for prayer in what has come to be called the Lord's Prayer (Matthew 6:6–13). This model prayer begins with an invocation followed by three petitions concerned with God and his glory. Next come three petitions concerned with man and his good. A doxology concludes this model prayer. Christ also set a pattern for the use of hymns of praise by singing with his disciples following the Last Supper (Matthew 26:30). In the Nazareth synagogue Christ set a pattern for the public reading and exposition of Scripture (Luke 4:16–27). He commanded the observance of baptism as part of our worship (Matthew 28:19). Christ as Head of the church established the Lord's Supper for continued use in the church (I Corinthians 11:23–25). Study of our Lord's earthly ministry reveals some of the content he desires in worship. Yet the church is not limited by that which Christ explicitly practiced during his earthly ministry. Our Lord has also revealed his will concerning worship in the Acts and the various epistles. All in all, we are not without the authoritative word of God in the matter of what constitutes proper Christian worship.

B. Christ directs the worship of the church through the gift of Scripture.

Jesus taught the regulative authority of Scripture for all of life. He was adamant in his rejection of any attempt to substitute human tradition for the divine commands of Scripture (Matthew 15:2–9; 21:12, 13; John 2:14–17). Once he confronted the Pharisees with the accusation, ''You nicely set aside the commandment of God in order to keep your tradition'' (Mark 7:9). It was the practice of the Pharisees to burden down the people of God with man-made laws while setting aside the clear teaching of God's commandments.

Instead of the burden of man-made laws we have the Scripture as a gift from Christ to his church and it alone is the authority which regulates all aspects of a believer's life. "All Scripture is inspired by God and profitable for teaching, for reproof, for correction, for training in righteousness, that the man of God may be adequate, equipped for every good work" (II Timothy 3:16, 17). The apostolic council is given to a young church leader, "I am writing these things to you...but in case I am delayed, I write so that you may know how one ought to conduct himself in the household of God, which is the church of the living God, the pillar and support of the truth" (I Timothy 3:14, 15). Because Scripture is designed as a regulative authority in the church and in all of life, the regulative principle of worship is a necessary corollary of accepting the full authority of Scripture. It reflects our conviction concerning Scripture's authority over the full spectrum of life.

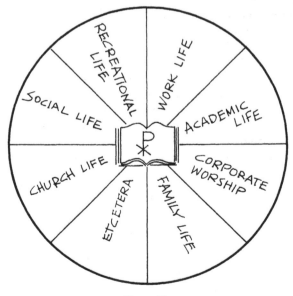

Figure19:
The Authority of Scripture in the Full Spectrum of Life

C. Christ directs the worship of the church through the normative standard that worship must be in spirit and in truth (John 4:19–24).

One morning as Jesus walked along the dusty roads of Sychar, a small town in Samaria, he paused to rest by Jacob's well, located in the center of the town. He soon initiated a conversation with a woman who had come to draw water. As the conversation progressed, Christ did some probing concerning her moral background and hit a nerve. The woman quickly attempted to divert the conversation to some technicalities of worship but Christ simply continued to teach this woman by discussing the topic she herself had introduced. The Holy Spirit has preserved this well-side conversation. An examination of it can help us know the mind of Christ concerning worship. What does he teach in this conversation?

First, Christ teaches that worship is no longer spatially restricted (John 4:19–21). The appropriate place of worship was an issue of contention between Jews and Samaritans. The Jews were convinced that the proper place for worship was the temple on Mount Zion in Jerusalem. The despised Samaritans couldn't disagree more. They believed that Mount Gerizim, located near Jacob's well, was definitely the proper place for worship.

Christ refused to take sides for Jerusalem or Mount Gerizim. Why? Because geography is not the central issue in worship. The hour of Christ's crucifixion and resurrection would dissolve the significance of geography. The centrality of the earthly Jerusalem would be eliminated. Believers from that time on would not need to assemble in the earthly Jerusalem but rather by faith they could enter the heavenly Jerusalem every time and at every place they gather for worship (Hebrews 12:18–24). The important thing now is not the physical locality but the spiritual reality — not *where* but *how*. Worship is not spatially restricted.

Second, worship — based in knowledge (John 4:22) — is to have a Godward focus (John 4:23). The focal point is not man and his needs but God and his glory. We give our worship to God the Father through the Son and with the help of the Spirit.

Our Lord is specific in emphasizing the worship of the Father. This indicates that the worship of God must be characterized by the particularity that exists in the Godhead. Worship must be offered in recognition of the trinitarian distinctions and to each person of the Godhead in accordance with his distinguishing properties and functions, especially as these are expressed in the economy of salvation.[1]

Third, worship is to be offered in spirit and in truth (John 4:24). What does it mean to worship in spirit? It is primarily referring to the human spirit. Worship is not to be confined to outward ceremony but is to be carried out with inner sincerity of heart. Elsewhere Christ explained, "This people honors Me with their lips, but their heart is far away from Me" (Matthew 15:8). Christ does not look for the mechanical movement of lips or bodies in elaborate ritual, but for the movement of the human spirit toward him in adoration and praise.

Have you ever attended a church service with problems or decisions weighing heavily on your mind? After ten or fifteen minutes you may have realized, "I just sang that hymn and read that Scripture but I don't have the slightest idea what I sang or read." In such a case as this it is clear that God has not been honored. The worshiper has not worshiped in spirit. The need is not for warm bodies to fill the pews, but for spirits in tune with the living God.

This kind of worship is difficult. How can you overcome the weakness of your spirit and bring forth genuine spiritual worship? By the help of the Holy Spirit! Worship in spirit is worship in and by and through the Holy Spirit who is active in worship. Philippians 3:3 refers to Christians as those " who worship in the Spirit of God." Ephesians 2:18 reminds us that "through Him [Christ] we both [Jews and Gentiles] have our access in one Spirit to the Father." It is the help of the Holy Spirit that enables believers to enter the Father's presence for worship. The Holy Spirit can motivate and empower believers to give God whole-hearted worship with all their spirit. The Holy Spirit is a Spirit of truth (John 14:17; 15:26; 16:13; I John 4:6) who desires worship that is in accord with the Holy Spirit — inspired Scripture rather than according to the devices of the human spirit.

Christ not only gave us the standard of worship in spirit. He directed us to give worship in truth. What does that mean? Some have suggested that worship in truth is worship that is not false. The first commandment states: "You shall have no other gods before Me" (Exodus 20:3). True worship has as its object the true God and him alone. Worship of saints, statues, heroes or anyone else is false. Yet there seems to be a more significant meaning to worship in truth. It means believers are to give worship that is in reality rather than in types and shadows. Under the old covenant worship involved a variety of symbolic offerings and objects that were anticipatory shadows of a reality to come. The truth they pointed to was Jesus Christ who fulfilled the Old Testament types and shadows. Now under the new covenant believers experience fulfilled worship through Jesus Christ who is the truth personified (John 14:6). To worship in truth is to worship in reality through Jesus Christ the truth rather than through Old Testament types and shadows.

Perhaps there's a further significance to worship in truth. Jesus said, "Thy word is truth" (John 17:17). Worship in truth is worship that is in agreement with Scripture which is God's truth.

So we see that Scripture has a regulative authority over our worship. The teaching of Christ supports the regulative principle of worship.

Figure 20:
Worship in Truth

71

IMPLEMENTATION
OF THE
REGULATIVE PRINCIPLE

The regulative principle has been defined as follows: "Since the Holy Scriptures are the only infallible rule of faith and practice, the principles of public worship must be derived from the Bible, and from no other source."[2] True worship includes only those elements derived from the Scripture. There must be biblical justification for all that one includes in worship. Introducing anything that is forbidden in Scripture or not derived from Scripture makes our worship false and unacceptable to God. The criteria in evaluating a service of worship must not be based upon pragmatism or tradition but the authoritative word of God. Everything introduced into worship must have either explicit or implicit biblical warrant.

How does one apply this principle? Perhaps a further qualification may help in the practical application of this standard. The regulative use of Scripture pertains to all that is a "part" of worship as distinguished from that which is merely a "circumstance" of worship. Believers must seek to determine the "parts" of worship from scriptural example and principle but it is not necessary to look for the "circumstances" of worship in Scripture. The Westminster Confession of Faith states: "There are some circumstances concerning the worship of God ... which are to be ordered by the light of nature, and Christian prudence, according to the general rules of the Word, which are always to be observed." (I:6). What are some examples of "circumstances" of worship that are not determinable from Scripture? They would include the length of the service, the hour of the assembly on Sunday, the form of the seating, and the material from which the pulpit is made. All such things are circumstances of worship which do not directly pertain to the regulative principle.

What then would be examples of "parts" of worship that would be unacceptable under the regulative principle? Some examples are given in the chart below:

Things forbidden in Scripture	Things not derived from Scripture
-images of Baal -visuals of deity -uninterpreted tongues	-praying to departed saints -pledges to national flags -carrying of carved crosses

Figure 21:
Unacceptable "Parts" of Worship

The regulative principle of worship is not to be used as a legalistic club to attack other believers. Not all who are convinced of this principle will agree on its application in a particular situation in the church. But it can prove to be a helpful guide in a day of free-wheeling liturgical experimentation. May it be your guide to offer God only that worship which is acceptable in his presence.

You may find it helpful to complete the chart project given below. List any "circumstances" of worship which you think are not "parts" of worship and therefore are not appropriate according to the regulative principle. Then list any "parts" of worship that you think are unacceptable because they are without biblical warrant. May our Sovereign Lord guide your thoughts as you desire to worship him acceptably in spirit and truth.

Circumstances of Worship	Unacceptable Parts of Worship	
	Things forbidden in Scripture	Things not derived from Scripture

Figure 22:
Application of the Regulative Principle

Questions for Review

1. Give some examples of ways Christ regulated the content of the church's worship. (Matthew 6:6–13; 26:30; Luke 4:16–27; Matthew 28:19; I Corinthians 11:23–25)

2. What is the relationship between our worship and the authority of the Bible? (Mark 7:7–9; II Timothy 3:16, 17; I Timothy 3:14, 15)

3. What did Christ teach about the location of worship? (John 4:19–21; Hebrews 12:18–24)

4. What did Christ teach about the foundation and focus of worship? (John 4:22, 23)

5. Explain what it means to worship in spirit and truth. (John 4:24; Matthew 15:8; Philippians 3:3; Ephesians 2:18; John 15:26; 16:13; Exodus 20:3; John 14:6; 17:17)

6. Define the regulative principle of worship and the distinction between circumstances and parts of worship.

Questions for Discussion

1. Do you believe the Westminster divines who drew up the Westminster Confession of Faith would agree with the way the regulative principle of worship is described in the chapter?

2. How would you answer someone who believed that the regulative principle was in operation under the old covenant but is no longer operative under the new covenant?

3. Suppose you were an elder of the church faced with a request from a member who wanted to do a tasteful dance interpretive of the Lord's Prayer in your worship service. What would you tell the person?

4. What are some examples of "circumstances" of worship?

5. What are some examples of "parts" of worship that are unacceptable?

6. How can one prevent the regulative principle of worship from becoming a divisive factor in the church?

[1] John Murray, "The Worship of God in the Four Gospels," *The Biblical Doctrine of Worship* (Pittsburgh: The Reformed Presbyterian Church of North America, 1974), p. 93.

[2] *The Standards of Government, Discipline and Worship of the Orthodox Presbyterian Church,* (Philadelphia: Committee on Christian Education, 1972), p. 66.

8

THE RIGHT INGREDIENTS

Biblical evidence is presented for including the following as parts of worship services: prayer, music, reading and exposition of Scripture, offerings, confessions of faith, the Lord's Supper, baptism, and benedictions.

Suppose you were in charge of the worship service in your church next Sunday and were given the freedom to add or delete anything from the usual order of service. You might try this with last Sunday's bulletin and a red pencil. What kinds of guidelines would you use to determine what should and should not be included in that service? You cannot find any prearranged order of service in the pages of the New Testament. *Scripture does not give us a prescribed liturgy but it does regulate the content of worship services.*

The regulative principle of worship states that true worship includes only that which has biblical warrant. Explicit or implicit biblical support must be found for all that forms a part of worship (as contrasted with a circumstance of worship). Biblical warrant may be found for several items that are discussed in this chapter.

PRAYER

It would be highly unusual to find a service of worship that was devoid of prayer. There is a reason for this. Christ gave believers a pattern for corporate prayer in the Lord's Prayer (Matthew 6:9–13). The New Testament church left believers an example of meeting for corporate prayer (Acts 2:42; 4:23ff.; 12:5). The Scripture is replete with examples of prayers in which the Father is addressed through the Son and with the aid of the Spirit. Biblical warrant is given for prayers of adoration, thanksgiving, confession, intercession, petition and dedication.

Many Christians regularly experience the difficulty of sitting through worship services struggling to stay awake during painfully long "pastoral prayers." Not only the length, but the stained-glass vocabulary of the minister often adds to the soporific effect of the prayer. Although prayers are not addressed to the congregation, each worshiper should be able to enter in and pray silently along with the one who is leading in prayer. It is the congregation's silent participation with the pastor which makes the prayer one of the whole church.

With respect to the congregation's participation in prayer, consider the word "amen" which is used to end both public and private prayers. "Amen" was originally a Hebrew word which has been directly carried over not only into English, but also into Italian, Spanish, French, German, Norwegian, Swedish, Danish and a host of other languages. Its use at the conclusion of a prayer is a way of confirming what was prayed and indicating one's desire that it "may be so in very truth." A vocal "amen" by a congregation at the end of a prayer can be stimulating. Whether one pronounces "ah-men" or "ay-men" is not as crucial as that the word be used intelligently and devotedly. To say "amen" meaningfully worshipers must silently participate in the prayers being offered and make them truly their own.

MUSIC

The Psalmist's invitation is, "Sing to the Lord a new song; sing to the Lord, all the earth" (96:1). Music has played a significant part in the life of the people of God from Old Testament times down through history. Christ in effect authorized the use of hymns in worship as he concluded the Last Supper by singing with his disciples (Matthew 26:30). The New Testament encourages the joyful singing of psalms, hymns and spiritual songs to the Lord out of the fullness of the Spirit (I Corinthians 14:26; Ephesians

5:18-20; Colossians 3:16). The singing need not be restricted to the one hundred and fifty psalms but may embrace any words which communicate the teaching of Scripture without contradicting biblical teaching. We have been given an example by Christ our Singer-Prophet. His singing before the Father is the highest worship and it was not limited to the one hundred and fifty psalms (Hebrews 2:12; cf. Romans 15:9; Ezra 3:11). One can also find evidence in the New Testament of hymns that were probably used in the early church. These include the "Magnificat" (Luke 1:46-55), "Benedictus" (Luke 1:68-79), "Gloria in Excelsis" (Luke 2:14), "Nunc Dimittis" (Luke 2:29-32) as well as a variety of other lesser known hymns (Revelation 4:8; Romans 11:33-36; I Timothy 1:17, 3:16; Ephesians 5:19; Philippians 2:6-11; Colossians 1:15-20; Hebrews 1:3).

Although music is an important part of corporate worship, it can easily be misused. Music can be enjoyed for its own sake in a way that fails to call attention to the triune God. The words of many commonly sung hymns major on human experience in a trite, sentimental way. All too often, hymns which are chosen for worship services are not directed to the triune God as expressions of praise for his attributes and acts. Frequently the music used in a service bears no relation to that which precedes or follows it. Our God deserves nothing but the best as we seek to offer to him music that honors his majestic name.

READING AND EXPOSITION OF SCRIPTURE

Scripture should be central in any service of worship. It is the basis upon which God reveals himself to us that we in turn might give him homage and service acceptable to God which is our "spiritual service of worship" (Romans 12:1).

The public reading of Scripture is commanded. "Give attention to the public reading of Scripture" (I Timothy 4:13). A precedent is found in the synagogue service where Christ read Scripture (Luke 4:16-21). Furthermore, many of the New Testament epistles were written to be read in the public assembly of the churches (Colos-

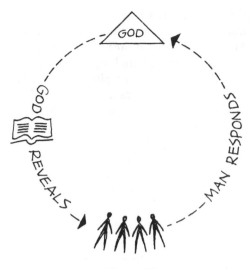

Figure 23:
Rhythm in the Service

sians 4:16; I Thessalonians 5:27; Philemon 2). Your appreciation of worship can be enhanced as you follow with an open Bible during the reading of God's word and participate in unison and responsive readings. Systematic exposure to the whole counsel of God, both Old and New Testaments, is essential in worship services. Some worshipers find it helpful to read the Scripture lessons in advance during the musical prelude. Scripture is to be approached as a vital communication from God to his people.

God also desires that his word be publicly preached and taught in the service of worship. The New Testament strongly bears this out with exhortations such as "Preach the word" (II Timothy 4:2; cf. I Timothy 4:6; 5:17; 6:2ff.; II Timothy 2:2; Titus 1:9). God has provided the office of pastor or teaching elder to insure that the whole counsel of God is faithfully preached (Ephesians 4:11, 12; I Timothy 3:2; 5:17). The central position of the pulpit in the room used for worship is not simply an architectural tradition or device to call attention to the preacher, but a reminder of the centrality of God's word in every service.

OFFERINGS

Did you ever wonder why an offering is taken in your church? Some regard the offering as an awkward interruption in the service—one that could best be eliminated. Others regard it as a pragmatic necessity to pay for utility bills, mortgages and ministers' salaries. Others manage to endure it by tossing in a loose dollar bill as the plate goes by, the same amount they have been giving during fifteen years of inflation. It can help to look upon the offering as an act of worship to God in response to who he is and what he has done. The monetary gifts of believers can be "a fragrant aroma, an acceptable sacrifice, well pleasing to God" (Philippians 4:18). In the early New Testament church, offerings appear to have been presented on a systematic, regular, proportional basis as the Christians met on the first day of each week (I Corinthians 16:1, 2; cf. II Corinthians 8 and 9). When you present offerings on the first day of the week it can be an outward, visible sign of the inward, spiritual offering of yourself with thankful heart (Romans 12:1, 2). You are privileged to join in honoring the Lord with your substance and the first fruits of all your increase (Proverbs 3:9). Will the ushers please come forward!

CONFESSIONS OF FAITH

How easy it is to rattle off the familiar Apostles' Creed without proper attention to its meaning. How easy it is to view it as an empty tradition or merely a time-filler in the service. Do Christians have any biblical warrant for using a public confession of faith as part of their worship? An affirmative answer can be found in Christ's good confession before Pilate. "Take hold of the eternal life to which you were called, and you made the good confession in the presence of many witnesses. I charge you in the presence of God, who gives life to all things, and of Jesus Christ, who testified the good confession before Pontius Pilate" (I Timothy 6:12, 13). The New Testament confessions center on the affirmation that "Jesus is Lord" (I Corinthians 12:3; cf. Romans 10:9, 10). More detailed confessions of faith are found scattered through the New Testament (I Corinthians 15:3–5; Romans 1:3, 4; 4:24, 25; 8:34;

Philippians 2:6–11; I Timothy 3:16; I Peter 3:18–22). Confessions of faith are used in worship as an opportunity for public affirmation of belief in the sound doctrines of Scripture and in the triune God. These confessions may include the historic creeds as well as the biblical affirmations. "Through [Jesus] then let us continually offer up a sacrifice of praise to God, that is, the fruit of lips that confess His name" (Hebrews 13:15). You may find it helpful in your private devotions to examine the component parts of the Apostles' Creed. Hold each part up to the light of Scripture and meditate on it so that you may recite it publicly with increased conviction.

THE LORD'S SUPPER

Most believers look forward to the celebration of the Lord's Supper. They realize that it was instituted by Christ in fulfillment of the old covenant Passover (Matthew 26:17; Mark 14:12; Luke 22:7). The Lord's Supper marked the initiation of the new covenant under which Christ was sacrificed as the unblemished Lamb of God (I Corinthians 11:25). The visible elements of bread and the fruit of the vine are used as a remembrance to "proclaim the Lord's death until He comes" (I Corinthians 11:26). One looks back on the once-for-all crucifixion as well as forward to the return of the resurrected Christ. The future anticipation is that of the gathering around the table at the heavenly banquet (Matthew 26:29; Mark 14:25; Luke 22:29, 30; John 6:54).

Figure 24:
The Looking Back and Forward of the Lord's Supper

The Lord's Supper is for believers only and is not a saving sacrament in itself. There is a vertical dimension as you feed on Christ's benefits and a horizontal dimension as you fellowship with other members of the one body of Christ. Thus it is a true "communion" service. "Is not the cup of blessing which we bless a sharing in the blood of Christ? Is not the bread which we break a sharing in the body of Christ? Since there is one loaf, we who are many are one body, for we all partake of the one loaf" (I Corinthians 10:16, 17).

Is the Lord really present in the communion? The answers historically given to this question may be summarized in the following chart.

Name of View	Description
Roman Catholic (transubstantiation)	Physical presence in the changed elements themselves
Lutheran (consubstantiation)	Physical presence in, under and along with the elements
Zwinglian (memorialism)	Elements are mere symbols of the work of Christ
Reformed	Real spiritual presence by faith through the Holy Spirit

Figure 25:
Views of the Lord's Presence

The Reformed view rejects any *physical* presence of Christ in the elements because his physical presence is at the right hand of the Father in heaven. However, there is a real spiritual presence of Christ by faith through the Holy Spirit (I Corinthians 10:16, 17). Communion is not a bare memorial as one might go to the cemetery and look at the symbol of the tombstone of a deceased relative and remember him or her. "Remember" is not a mental exercise alone but an actual dynamic recalling of the crucified and risen Christ who is spiritually present and actually appropriated by believers in faith as they meet in assembly. "They that worthily communicate feed upon his body and blood to their spiritual nourishment and growth in grace; have their union and communion with him confirmed'' (Westminster Larger Catechism, Question 168).

BAPTISM

The sacrament of baptism has tragically been a source of division among Christians. Arguments over the mode and subjects of baptism have occupied scholars for generations. The purpose of this chapter is not to resolve these arguments but rather to show the warrant for including baptism as part of one's worship. Christ commanded baptism to be administered in the name of the triune God (Matthew 28:19). It is an outward visible sign and seal of spiritual reality and is to be administered before the assembled Christian community. Its significance can perhaps be best explained according to the trinitarian formula.

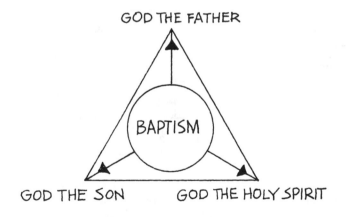

Figure 26:
The Sign and Seal of Baptism

Baptism is a sign of union with God the Father. It is a sign of initiation into the covenant people of God corresponding to the Old Testament sign of circumcision (Colossians 2:11, 12). Baptism is a sign of union with God the Son who was crucified and resurrected and who washes away sin (Romans 6:2–6; Galatians 3:27, 28; Colossians 2:12; Acts 22:16). Baptism is also a sign of union with the Holy Spirit who baptizes (I Corinthians 12:13; Ephesians 4:5). Thus baptism is an important part of the worship that should occur as God's covenant people assemble in his name.

BENEDICTIONS

Goodbyes can be difficult. Walk through a busy airport and you can see husbands and wives in parting embraces, children waving goodby to grandparents, and lovers fighting back tears as they part. Farewells seem to be an inevitable reality of human existence, even for worshipers. When God's people meet in his presence and in the fellowship of one another, the time comes to say farewell. Usually this farewell is called a benediction. These last words of the service are a farewell blessing in which God's name is placed on his people who leave corporate worship to scatter and worship him in all they do and say throughout the week (Romans 12:1; Colossians 3:17).

Biblical warrant for use of a benediction is found in the Aaronic blessing of the Old Testament priests who invoked God's name with uplifted hands (Numbers 6:22–27). This practice was carried over into the synagogue. Christ also blessed his disciples with uplifted hands at his ascension (Luke 24:50–53). Your minister as God's representative raises his hands and pronounces: "The grace of the Lord Jesus Christ, and the love of God, and the fellowship of the Holy Spirit, be with you all" (II Corinthians 13:14). "Amen."

You might use the teaching in this chapter to engage in a follow-through project. You recall that the principle taught in this chapter is that Scripture does not give us a prescribed liturgy but it does regulate the content of worship services. Find a copy of a church bulletin and examine each item included in the order of service. See if you can explain the significance of each part of the service. What biblical teaching can you give to help explain each part? The discipline of thinking through these items can help increase your appreciation for corporate worship this coming Sunday.

Questions for Review

1. What is the significance of "Amen" at the conclusion of prayers? (I Corinthians 14:16; Romans 1:25; 15:33; 16:25–27)

2. What are the biblical reasons for which singing is included in worship services? (Psalm 96:1; Matthew 26:30; Ephesians 5:18–20; Colossians 3:16)

3. Summarize the place Scripture should occupy in worship services. (I Timothy 4:13; Luke 4:16–21; Colossians 4:16; I Thessalonians 5:27; Philemon 2; II Timothy 2:2; 4:2; I Timothy 4:6; 5:17; 6:2ff.; Titus 1:9; Ephesians 4:11, 12)

4. Why should offerings be included in worship services? (Philippians 4:18; I Corinthians 16:1, 2; II Corinthians 8, 9; Romans 12:1, 2; Proverbs 3:9)

5. What is the biblical justification for using confessions of faith? (I Timothy 6:12, 13; Hebrews 13:15)

6. How is the Lord's Supper a "true communion service"? (I Corinthians 10:16, 17)

7. What is the significance of baptism according to the trinitarian formula? (Matthew 28:19; Galatians 3:13–17; Colossians 2:11, 12; Romans 6:2–6; Galatians 3:27, 28; Acts 22:16; I Corinthians 12:13; Ephesians 4:5)

8. What biblical justification is there for using a benediction in a service? (Numbers 6:22–27; Luke 24:50–53; II Corinthians 13:14; Hebrews 13:20, 21)

Questions for Discussion

1. What are the advantages and disadvantages of a congregation using vocal "amens" in a service?

2. What kinds of music do you think would be wrong to include in

a Sunday morning worship service in your church?

3. What are the differences in textual, topical, and expository preaching and which do you prefer? Why?

4. What suggestions would you give to a young man who has just graduated from seminary and is about to start preaching regularly?

5. Are there any ways of taking the offering other than the present practice in your church?

6. How can one avoid the problem of worshipers repeating a confession of faith mechanically rather than in spirit and truth?

7. How often should the Lord's Supper be celebrated?

8. Are there any additional "parts" of worship that may be biblically included but were not mentioned in this chapter?

9

SPILLOVER OF JOY

This chapter shows how worship services should have a doxological note of joy and how worship should spill over from the Christian sabbath to all the days of the week. A summary of the biblical theology of worship follows with guide questions to facilitate its implementation.

People watching can be fascinating. Have you ever used the time while waiting in an airport terminal to study the crowds of people passing by? You would probably observe a potpourri of sizes, ages, dress and facial expressions. The fact that the study of people is intriguing was evident in the success of the television program "Candid Camera."

Suppose you had a one-way glass with which to observe a Sunday morning worship service in your church. What would you see on the faces of the congregation and what conclusions could you draw? Some faces might be etched with anxiety because of crumbling marriages or threatened jobs. Other faces might convey boredom as the worshipers daydream about being somewhere else. Faces often reflect the inner circumstances of the wearer. How easy it is to allow the circumstances and problems of one's life to influence one's frame of mind during a service of worship. For example, an argument in the car on the way to a church service can send the whole service down the tubes for some people. It may prove helpful to keep the following theological principle in mind.

WORSHIP SHOULD HAVE A DOXOLOGICAL NOTE OF JOYFUL PRAISE TO THE TRIUNE GOD

Outward circumstances can dampen one's joy in worship, yet God expects that corporate worship be a joyful experience. Believers are to enter God's holy presence not only with reverence but also with a doxological note of joy as praise is offered to God the Father through Jesus Christ by the power of the Holy Spirit. This is not to suggest that one needs to conjure up an artificial joy that is contrary to reality but rather that believers have real, substantial cause for making worship a joyful occasion.

Jesus Christ is the prime reason for joy in corporate worship. The praise so evident in the Old Testament psalms and temple worship can be even greater under the new covenant because Christ has come to bring fulfillment. Believers no longer need to worship in the shadows and types of the old covenant but can now worship in very truth through Jesus Christ (John 4:24). No wonder the first advent of Christ evoked such ripples of joy on earth: "Joy to the world, the Lord has come." Joy filled the hills and valleys in the environs of Bethlehem on the night of the Messiah's birth. "And suddenly there appeared with the angel a multitude of the heavenly host praising God, and saying, 'Glory to God in the highest, and on earth peace among men with whom He is pleased' " (Luke 2:13, 14).This angelic song known as the "Gloria in Excelsis" has been sung by the church for generations. Christians sing it not only at Christmas but also during the summer months and when the smell of burning leaves fills the autumn air. It is appropriate to rejoice year-round because Jesus the Messiah has come in fulfillment. Christians have reason to proclaim joyfully:

> Glory to God in the highest,
>   and peace to his people on earth.
> Lord God, heavenly King,
> almighty God and Father,
>   we worship you, we give you thanks,
>   we praise you for your glory.

A further reason for joy centers around the person of the Holy Spirit. The fillings of the Holy Spirit during the age following the baptism at Pentecost make possible an overflow of joy that should be evident in worship services. Christ said, " 'He who believes in Me, as the Scripture said, "From his innermost being shall flow rivers of living water." ' But this He spoke of the Spirit, whom those who believed in Him were to receive" (John 7:38, 39). Should not this be reflected in today's church services? "The kingdom of God is not eating and drinking, but righteousness and peace and joy in the Holy Spirit" (Romans 14:17). So joy need not be a conjured-up, artificial emotion but it is a natural reality based on the coming of Christ, the fulfillment, and the Holy Spirit, the filler with joy.

This is not to be misinterpreted as a plea for irreverent ecstasy with free-for-all expressions in services. The majestic God is to be approached with reverence in the beauty of holiness. But reverence need not always be identified with somberness, long faces and hushed whispers. Worship can be simultaneously reverent and joyful.

How can this joyful praise be reflected in services? Music can be a most appropriate way of expressing our joy before God: "With psalms and hymns and spiritual songs, singing with thankfulness in your hearts to God" (Colossians 3:16). (See also Ephesians 5:19 and Romans 15:11.)

Music can be an effective means to express joy to our listening God. Prayers likewise should contain a doxological note. The New Testament is replete with examples of this (Romans 1:25; 9:5; 11:33–36; 16:27; Galatians 1:5; Ephesians 3:20, 21; Philippians 4:20; I Timothy 1:17; 6:15, 16; II Timothy 4:18; Hebrews 13:20, 21; I Peter 4:11; 5:11; Jude 24, 25; Revelation 1:5, 6; 5:13, 14). Try looking up these references, jotting down the phrases, and then using some of them in your prayers.

Generally there is more enthusiasm in the grandstands of a sports arena than in the pews of the church. Obviously not all the antics of popcorn-crunching, fist-waving sports fans are appropriate for an assembly before the Majestic One. Yet if worshipers are doing more than playing church, shouldn't it be evident in facial expressions and actions that reflect the joy of praising God?

WORSHIP SHOULD SPILL OVER
FROM THE LORD'S DAY TO
ALL THE DAYS OF THE WEEK

The parking lot of most churches is usually vacant from Monday through Saturday. Yet drive by on Sunday morning and you will see Buicks, Fords and Toyotas by the score. Why has the Christian church singled out Sunday as *the* day of corporate worship? Is it no more than a cultural tradition passed on by the Puritans of early New England? Scripture tells us that at creation God established one day out of seven as a sabbath (Genesis 2:2, 3). This creation ordinance was reaffirmed in the moral law of the Decalogue (Exodus 20:8–11) and this fourth commandment is still operative today. However the time of the sabbath has shifted from the seventh day to the first day of the week in recognition of the resurrection of the Lord of the church (Matthew 28:1). The Westminster Confession of Faith explains,

> "By a positive, moral, and perpetual commandment binding all men in all ages, he hath particularly appointed one day in seven, for a Sabbath, to be kept holy unto him: which, from the beginning of the world to the resurrection of Christ, was the last day of the week; and, from the resurrection of Christ, was changed into the first day of the week, which, in Scripture, is called the Lord's Day, and is to be continued to the end of the world, as the Christian sabbath." (XXI.7)

The early church faithfully observed the first day of the week for corporate worship (Acts 20:7; I Corinthians 16:2; Revelation 1:10). Believers are given freedom as to the time of the day they meet for worship and as to the length of the service but not as to the day of the week. Christians are to meet for corporate praise on the Lord's day. However, worship need not be locked up in a compartment named "Sunday" that is opened only once a week. Why?

The New Testament teaches that worship should spill over from the Lord's day to all the days of the week. The early Christians met not only on Sundays but it is said of some that every day they

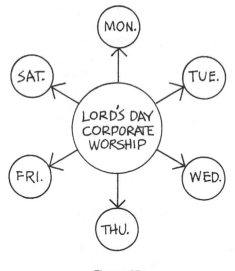

Figure 27:
Worship Spillover

continued to meet together (Acts 2:42, 46). Even when you are not assembled with other believers, you can be involved in worship in that everything you do can be an act of worship performed to the glory of God. This truth is evident in the New Testament use of *latreia,* the common Greek word for worship.

Latreia is used in the Old Testament Septuagint primarily for sacrificial acts performed in the tabernacle and temple. In the New Testament, however, its use broadens to embrace the whole of life which is a service or worship done to the glory of God. For example, Paul calls his mission work in general an offering of worship to God (Romans 1:9). Then he urges believers "by the mercies of God, to present your bodies a living and holy sacrifice, acceptable to God, which is your spiritual service of worship [*latreia*]" (Romans 12:1). Paul also reminds us: "Whatever you do in word or deed, do all in the name of the Lord Jesus, giving thanks through Him to God the Father" (Colossians 3:17). So the full spectrum of life is lived before God and is offered up as an act of worship to his glory. The Westminster Shorter Catechism summarizes all of this in one brief statement: "Man's chief end is to glorify God and enjoy him forever.'' You can worship God in your job at an office or factory, by serving on a community committee, by planting a garden or playing a musical instrument. This does not negate the importance of corporate worship on the Lord's day but rather it prepares you for corporate praise. The Sunday assembly in turn should send you forth eager to glorify God in the situations that occur during the ensuing week. True worship cannot be isolated from all we are in life nor can true living be isolated from worship.

UTILIZATION OF THEOLOGICAL PRINCIPLES

Have you ever sat through one of those so-called worship services which consist of a plodding routine of hymns-announcements-offering-sermon? Nothing seems to fit together and there is no evidence of a theology of worship. The congregation can barely give a one-sentence definition of worship much less articulate its theology. An urgent need exists in the contemporary church to teach and apply the biblical theology of worship. This book has been written with this need in mind. The theological principles covered in these first nine chapters may be summarized and illustrated by Figure 28.

Theology is not intended to be abstractly impractical but is to form a foundation for all one does in the church. The principles discussed in this book can be used in a practical way to evaluate corporate worship in a church. You may find it helpful to reflect on the questions below — questions that are based on the biblical theology of worship — and consider their relevance for the service of worship in your church.

1. Does this service have content rooted in God's revelation of his name, glory, acts and attributes?

2. Does this service make one aware of the presence of the triune God among his assembled people?

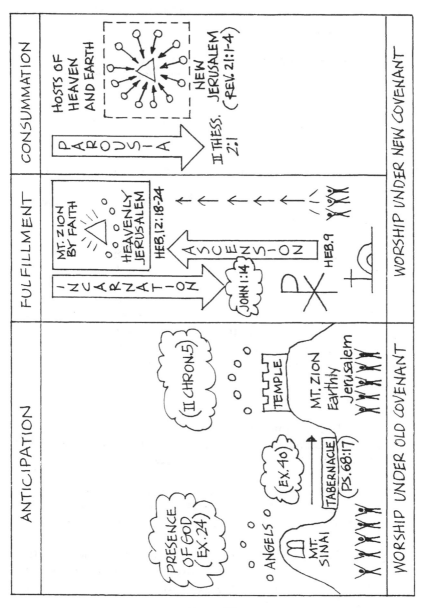

Figure 28:
Biblical Theology of Worship

3. Does this service reflect the fulfillment Christ has brought under the new covenant?

4. Does this service convey the reality that the earthly holy ones are assembled by faith with the heavenly angels in heavenly worship through Christ?

5. Does this service conform to the regulative principle with biblical warrant for all its parts?

6. Does this service encourage worship that is in spirit and truth?

7. Does this service reflect a joyful note of doxological praise to the triune God?

8. Does this service create an overflow that spills over into the daily lives of the worshipers?

Try re-reading these questions to see if there are any changes you wish to make in your experience of corporate worship. Church leaders and worship committees might find them useful in periodic evaluation of the church's worship in an effort to give the triune God the very best worship — of which he is supremely worthy.

Questions for Review

1. What are two main reasons for which worship should have a doxological note of joyful praise to the triune God? (John 4:24; Luke 2:13, 14; John 7:38, 39; Romans 14:7)

2. What are two ways of expressing joy in corporate worship? (Colossians 3:16; Ephesians 5:19; Romans 15:11; 9:5; 11:33–36; 16:27; Galatians 1:5; Ephesians 3:20, 21; Philippians 4:20)

3. What are the reasons for the celebration of the sabbath on Sunday? (Genesis 2:2, 3; Exodus 20:8–11; Matthew 28:1; Acts 20:7; I Corinthians 16:2; Revelation 1:10)

4. What is the significance of the term *latreia*? Check it out in a

good concordance.

5. What is the relation between Sunday worship and the other six days of the week? (Colossians 3:17)

Questions for Discussion

1. What can Christians do to prevent outward circumstances from dampening their joy in worship?

2. Is the balance between a somberness and joyfulness in services merely a matter of cultural tastes and backgrounds?

3. Why does there seem to be little genuine enthusiasm in some worship services?

4. Give some examples of ways believers can worship God in the full spectrum of daily life.

5. Give some examples of ways one's theology of worship affects one's practice of worship.

3

The History of
Christian Worship

10

KNOW YOUR ROOTS

Post-apostolic era worship during the first four centuries is surveyed as well as developments in the subsequent Middle Ages. The dominant liturgical trends of the medieval church as it moved away from Scripture reveal some helpful lessons for the contemporary church.

The bell rings to mark the commencement of the freshman history class. The instructor begins to drone on in a dull monotone about irrelevancies of a bygone era. You can see some of the students nod and struggle to keep their eyes open. At the end of the period the teacher administers a brief review quiz in which the students are asked to give pertinent information such as the color of Napoleon's horse and the date of his wedding anniversary. This is the stereotype that some people have concerning the study of history.

The foregoing characterization does not need to be true. The proper study of history can be extremely helpful in giving perspective. Those who fail to study the past are prone to repeat its mistakes unnecessarily. This is true in the area of Christian worship. Study of the church's past history can help one to avoid the pitfalls of historical provincialism and can enrich one's experience of corporate worship. It is with these convictions in view that this chapter proceeds.

POST-APOSTOLIC WORSHIP (the first four centuries)

Suppose you were a Christian living in the period immediately following the death of the apostles. What would your experience of worship be like? You couldn't go to the yellow pages to look up the address of the local church. You couldn't even look for steeples or stained-glass windows because Christians met in homes for worship. Church buildings were not constructed until the fourth century under the Roman emperor Constantine who adopted Christianity as the official religion of the state. Until this time groups of believers assembled in homes on Sundays. The format of these worship services was rather simple and unadorned. A revealing glimpse is given in Justin Martyr's *Apology* written around A.D. 150.

> On the day called Sunday there is a gathering together in the same place of all who live in a city or a rural district. The memoirs of the apostles or the writings of the prophets are read, as long as time permits. Then when the reader ceases, the president in a discourse admonishes and urges the imitation of these good things. Next we all rise together and send up prayers. And, as I said before, when we cease from our prayer, bread is presented and wine and water. The president in the same manner sends up prayers and thanksgiving according to his ability, and the people sing out their assent saying the 'Amen.' A distribution and participation of the elements for which thanks have been given is made to each person, and to those who are not present it is sent by the deacons. Those who have means and are willing, each according to his own choice, gives what he wills, and what is collected is deposited with the president. He provides for the orphans and widows, those who are in want on account of sickness or some other case, those who are in bonds and strangers who are sojourning, and in a word he becomes the protector of all who are in need.[1]

See how many of the parts of worship discussed in chapter 8 appear in this account by Justin Martyr.

Several liturgical developments occurred during this post-apostolic era. First, there was movement from simplicity to more fixed and elaborate forms of liturgy. This included the gradual development of specific rules on how to conduct various services. For example, the *Didache*, a Christian document from the late first or early second century, enumerated the following rules for baptisms:

> Having first rehearsed all these things, baptize in the name of the

102

Father and of the Son and of the Holy Ghost in living water. But if you have not living water, baptize into other water; and, if thou canst not in cold, in warm. If you have neither, pour water thrice on the head in the name . . . Before the baptism let the baptizer and the baptized fast, and others if they can.[2]

Further development occurred as the church began to compile lectionaries—lists of prescribed Scripture readings to be used weekly in each church. It was also during this period that the church year calendar was first developed. The initial focus on Christmas and Easter was expanded as an increasing number of holy days and seasons were added.

Second, the post-apostolic era saw a move toward an increasing Old Testament emphasis in worship services. This was especially evident in changing views of the Lord's Supper which began to be viewed as an offering to God more than a meal of fellowship. Writings such as the *Didache* began using Malachi 1:11–14 in connection with the Lord's Supper. Malachi wrote, " 'From the rising of the sun, even to its setting, My name will be great among the nations, and in every place incense is going to be offered to My name, and a grain offering that is pure; for My name will be great among the nations,' says the Lord of hosts. But you are profaning it, in that you say, 'The table of the Lord is defiled . . .' " Malachi was not referring to the Lord's Supper or the communion table but to the table in the temple on which animals were placed in preparation for Old Testament animal sacrifices under the ceremonial law. The misapplication of Malachi 1:11–14 was only part of a slow drift away from the apostolic teaching of New Testament worship. It was also during this period that the church began referring to the communion table as an altar.

What happens when you enter a morning worship service in most churches today? The usher greets you and hands you a bulletin that lists the order of service. There were no mimeographed bulletins used in the post-apostolic era. The earliest record we have of an order of service is called the Clementine Liturgy. It was used by Christians who met in Antioch around A.D. 380 and may be fairly representative of the simplicity of early worship.

Liturgy of the Word
Scripture readings
Sermon
Prayers
Kiss of peace

Liturgy of the Upper Room
Bringing of bread and wine
Eucharistic prayer
The communion

MEDIEVAL WORSHIP (A.D. 400–1520)

The few seeds of deviation from biblical worship that were sown in the post-apostolic era began to bloom during the Middle Ages. Several unhealthy trends developed and created problems that eventually led to the Reformation. An awareness of these problems can serve today as a corrective for any tendencies to move in the same direction.

What were these dominant liturgical trends during the Middle Ages? First, the church began to conduct services in languages other than the people's own language. The reason for this was that Christianity began to spread geographically to new areas beyond the Roman and Greek cultures. The church then attempted to carry the worship of the old countries into new cultures without making the necessary cultural adjustments. Services were still held in Greek and Latin with the assumption that people in the new countries would learn the language. This proved to be a faulty assumption. The use of Latin and Greek created a sense of mystery in services but it hindered people from worshiping with understanding (cf. John 4:22–27; Matthew 22:37). If you have ever sat through a service in Latin you can appreciate the problems of attempting to worship when the language is not in your vernacular. In fact, this pattern that began in the Middle Ages persisted in the Roman church until the Second Vatican Council of 1962–1965. At that time the decision was made to abandon the Old Latin mass and replace it with the vernacular of the locale. This has corrected a medieval problem although it has not occurred without the strident protests of some conservatives in the Roman church.

A second medieval trend was a failure to give the people instruction that would enable them to enter into meaningful worship in spirit and truth. Rather than giving clear biblical teaching, the church began to stress visual devices. For example, the Second Council of Nicaea in A.D. 787 endorsed the use of statues, icons and paintings as valid parts of worship. People could enter the church buildings and see biblical events portrayed in graphic murals. They could see and touch impressive statues of saints and apostles—even of Christ—thus supposedly compensating for a lack of biblical teaching and a service they could not understand. The aesthetic and emotional elements were encouraged to such an extent that worship became virtually synonymous with the ornate and awe-inspiring. The church had clearly moved away from the teaching of the second commandment and its regulation of worship. "You shall not make for yourself an idol, or any likeness of what is in heaven above or on the earth beneath or in the water under the earth. You shall not worship them or serve them" (Exodus 20:4, 5). The Heidelberg Catechism explains: "God cannot and may not be visibly portrayed in any way. Although creatures may be portrayed, yet God forbids making or having such images if one's intention is to worship them or to serve God through them" (Question 97). The Catechism goes on to ask (Question 98): "But may not images be permitted in the churches as teaching aids for the unlearned?" And answers: "No, we shouldn't try to be wiser than God. He wants his people instructed by the living preaching of his Word—not by idols that cannot even talk."

A third trend was the development of the mass to the point where a disproportionate emphasis was placed upon the sacrament to the neglect of the word of God. The church began to look on the mass as a resacrifice of Christ on a literal altar even though the Scripture teaches that Jesus no longer makes sacrifices because he offered himself as the supreme sacrifice once and for all (see Hebrews 7:26, 27). The physical elements were elevated and worshiped since they were assumed to be transformed into the physical body and blood of Christ. This doctrine of transubstantiation developed to the point where it was authoritatively formulated as church dogma at the Lateran Council in A.D. 1215. Accompanying these doctrinal shifts was the movement of the altar to a distance from the people thus increasing their sense of non-participation. The mass became a spectacle viewed by the people with increasing use of visuals, incense and symbolic movements by the celebrating priests. The priesthood of every believer was being ignored and the preaching of the word of God was being neglected (cf. I Peter 2:5; Revelation 1:6).

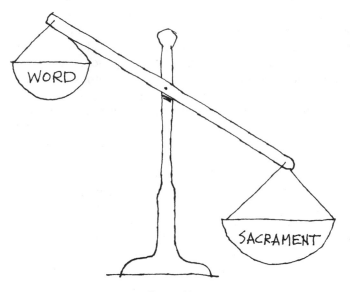

Figure 29:
Medieval Word/Sacrament Imbalance

If you had visited a worship service in the Middle Ages in the West you would have found an order of service similar to the following:

Liturgy of the Word
Mass of the Catechumens (recital of Psalm 43,
mutual confession, prayers)
Kyrie
Epistle, Alleluia, Gospel
Nicene Creed

Liturgy of the Faithful
Offertory
Canon to Benedictus
Prayers for the church
Prayers of oblation and consecration
Narrative of the institution and anamnesis
Consignation and elevation
Fraction and commixture
Communion
Prayers, thanksgiving, dismissal

A study of the history of Christian worship in the Middle Ages reveals some important lessons for the contemporary church. Christians need to beware of the human tendency to add to the liturgy ritual, artistic flourishes, aesthetic touches and human traditions that are without biblical warrant. This can easily happen when the regulative principle of worship is set aside.

Picture this: On the Feast of Epiphany a service was being conducted in a liturgical Protestant church. It was a visually stimulating service, the sanctuary having been filled with carved statues and flaming candles. The processional began with a man holding high a golden, carved symbol, followed by clergy and choir garbed in beautifully colored robes adorned with ecclesiastical symbols. Throughout the service a golden censer on a chain was used to fill the sanctuary with the aroma of incense. The music was a delightful harmonization of trumpets, choir and stately pipe organ. All the senses were stimulated, making the celebration a very moving aesthetic and emotional experience. But for many it was a shallow spiritual experience. The regulative principle had been ignored as multiple human additions to worship substituted aesthetic and emotional excitement for spiritual reality. This problem began in the Middle Ages and, sadly, is repeated in some places today.

Another lesson from the Middle Ages is that we need to be careful to maintain the balance between word and sacrament. The sacrament must not be allowed to swallow up the word. We are not to celebrate the Lord's Supper divorced from the proper reading and preaching of the word of God.

Furthermore, we need to beware of allowing a worship service to become a passive spectacle for the congregation rather than a time of active participation by each worshiper. The priesthood of every believer which was denied in the Middle Ages should not be forgotten in our day. This historical study has also pinpointed another area to which the contemporary church should give attention. We need to insure that adequate teaching is given in the Christian church in order that worship may be understood by all Christians. Faithful expository preaching of Scripture is needed. Teaching on the biblical theology of worship should also occur in the church. Let us not repeat the mistakes of the past!

At the end of this book several suggestions are given for further reading. You may find it helpful to locate one of those books and read it with the intent of increasing your understanding of the doctrine and history of Christian worship. The church needs informed worshipers. May you be one of them!

Questions for Review

1. When did Christians begin meeting in church buildings for worship?

2. What were some of the worship trends that developed during the post-apostolic era?

3. How did the use of services in Greek and Latin rather than in the people's vernacular originate and what effect did it have?

4. Why was there a multiplication of statues, icons and paintings in churches during the Middle Ages?

5. How did the church's view of the Lord's Supper change during the Middle Ages?

6. Name some lessons one can learn from the history of worship in the Middle Ages.

Questions for Discussion

1. Of what value is it for Christians to look at the history of worship in the church?

2. Look at the order of the Clementine Liturgy and explain which elements you think should and should not be included in a worship service today. Is there anything missing?

3. Can you give any examples of cultural adaptations in liturgy that missionaries should make in moving into new cultures?

4. What are some specific ways in which the church can teach her members so they are able to enter into worship in spirit and truth?

5. What should the church do to avoid the harmful tendency to add to worship by ritual and human traditions that are contrary to Scripture?

¹Justin Martyr, *Apology*, I: 65–67; cited by Henry Bettenson, *Documents of the Christian Church,* (London: Oxford University Press, 1963), pp. 94, 95.

²*The Didache,* VII; cited by Bettenson, p. 90.

11

REFORMATION COMES

This chapter shows the conditions that led to the Reformation and it surveys the contributions of Luther, Zwingli and Calvin to the needed reform of the church's liturgy.

Sweeping changes were made in the liturgy of the church during the sixteenth and seventeenth centuries. God raised up men in Europe and Britain who called the church back to biblical doctrine, practice and worship. The reverberations from these changes encircled the globe and are still being felt today. The changes were not only theological but liturgical as well. If the Reformation had not occurred, your Sundays would undoubtedly be quite different from what they are today. How grateful Christians should be for the rich heritage of the Reformation and its effects on church liturgy.

THE NEED FOR REFORMATION OF CHURCH WORSHIP

Was the Reformation really necessary? If you could jump into a time capsule and participate in a worship service in the early fifteen hundreds you would undoubtedly be convinced of the need for reformation. You would discover that the entire service was in Latin instead of in the vernacular of the people. Scripture readings and prayers probably would be unintelligible to you (cf. Matthew 22:37). Your eyes would behold a sanctuary full of ornate statues, carved crosses, and religious paintings which, though aesthetically delightful, could prove spiritually distracting (cf. Exodus 20:4). You would see elaborate visual drama enacted by priests while you and the other worshipers passively looked on at a distance (cf. I Peter 2:5). The central part of the service would be the resacrifice of Christ, the supposed transformation of wine and wafer into his physical body and blood (cf. Hebrews 10:12). Very little emphasis, if any, would be given to preaching or teaching of the word of God (cf. I Timothy 4:13). You would also discover the confusing addition of many feast days into an elaborate church year calendar (cf. Colossians 2:16). The need would be evident for a reforming purge of unwarranted accretions. This need did not go unnoticed as God sovereignly worked to raise up men who boldly championed biblical reformation of the medieval church.

MARTIN LUTHER'S CONTRIBUTION

A son was born to a poor German miner and his wife on November 10, 1483. He grew out of humble surroundings into a position where he revolutionized the church by proclaiming justification by faith in Christ alone. The ecclesiastical turmoil he generated reached a climax at the famous Diet of Worms where the Emperor Charles V called Luther to judgment for his radical views. Subsequent generations of Christians have thrilled at the retelling of the story of that assembly before whom Luther proclaimed, "I can neither, nor dare retract anything, for my conscience is captive to the Word of God . . .. Here I stand. I can do no other. So help me God. Amen."

This bold Reformer made some noteworthy contributions to the improvement of church worship. He rejected the idea of the mass being a resacrifice of Christ because this view conflicted with the doctrine of justification by faith alone. In place of transubstantiation he taught what came to be called consubstantiation, the view that the real physical presence of Christ is under, with and alongside the elements. Luther wrote in his *Small Catechism* that the sacrament of the altar "is the true body and blood of our Lord Jesus Christ under the bread and wine." He also boldly translated the Latin service into the German vernacular of the people. In his *Formula Missae* of 1523 he called on German poets to prepare suitable hymns so God's people might join in praising the Lord in their own native tongue. Soon churches were ringing with the voices of worshipers singing hymns written by Luther himself. These included "A Mighty Fortress Is Our God," "Saviour of the

Nations, Come," "Christ Jesus Lay in Death's Strong Bands," "All Praise to Thee, Eternal Lord" and countless others that may be found in the index of most hymnals.

Some people who visit a Lutheran church today come away remarking, "That's almost like a Roman Catholic service!" The sanctuary may have a variety of religious symbols, an altar and burning candles. The clergy, robed in liturgical garb, lead the congregation in a ritual in some ways resembling the Roman rite. This is understandable in light of the influence of Martin Luther who seemed to be the most conservative of the Reformers in the area of liturgical change. He retained some ceremonies, vestments and symbols because he believed that certain things could be accepted as part of worship unless they were specifically forbidden in Scripture. This lack of adherence to the regulative principle accounts for the retention of some medieval elements in his liturgy. Nevertheless one can be thankful for his positive accomplishments.

ULRICH ZWINGLI'S CONTRIBUTION

With catchy illustrations and humor such that people were actually known to laugh in the cathedral in Zurich, Switzerland, Ulrich Zwingli was the preacher who dared to break the somberness of medieval worship. However, not everyone found Zwingli amusing. In 1523 he wrote *Commentary on True and False Religion* which called for the total abolition of the Roman mass. He proceeded to do that very thing in the Zurich cathedral by removing all artistic additions such as images, choirs, organs and any use of music. Religious murals on the walls were whitewashed away. He wanted to recover the simplicity of New Testament worship which he believed should appeal to the mind rather than to the senses.

Zwingli also radically altered the content of worship services. He took the pulpit for the first time on his thirty-fifth birthday and startled the congregation by announcing that he would not give the traditional homily based on the Roman lectionary reading. Instead he would begin preaching straight through the New Testament. He eliminated the weekly celebration of the Lord's Supper and replaced it with quarterly observance. On Maundy Thursday, 1525, he did what no priest had done for hundreds of years. Ignoring the high altar, he stepped out of the pulpit and stood behind a simple table on which were placed wooden beakers and plates. After praying in the language of the people he gave the elements to men who distributed them from pew to pew. This sounds rather commonplace for us but was most revolutionary at that time and place in history. Zwingli rejected the Roman view of transubstantiation and instead taught a view known as memorialism in which the Lord's Supper is not a means of grace but a teaching occasion in which the elements cause us to remember the past death of Christ. This Zwinglian view has strongly shaped the understanding of many contemporary evangelicals.

Zwingli developed a new order of service modeled after the medieval *prone*. The *prone* was a service that was developed in the late Middle Ages to bring more teaching into the mass. It was a teaching service which was held before the regular mass. The basic order was: Invocation, Scripture reading in Latin and the vernacular, Sermon, Intercession, Lord's Prayer with paraphrase of each clause, Apostles' Creed and Ten Commandments. Zwingli took the basic structure of this *prone,* translated it into the vernacular, and used it in his church in Zurich. The sermon was dominant and the people were mainly passive. It has been suggested that this is the historic antecedent of the modern preaching service in which the sermon is central and everything else tends to be looked upon as preliminaries.

The later Puritans of England and New England likewise emphasized a preaching service in which the other parts were pushed to the background. For example, in early New England sermons would last two to three hours. This meant that some struggled to stay awake and others would simply exit in the middle of the sermon. In an attempt to discourage his parishioners from leaving early, one New England minister announced one Sunday that he would preach the first part of his sermon to the sinners and the latter part to the saints. He said that the sinners would of course be free to leave after their portion had been delivered. That announcement solved the problem of departing parishioners. Every single soul remained until the end of that sermon!

JOHN CALVIN'S CONTRIBUTION

John Calvin was born in France on July 10, 1509, after Zwingli had already passed from the scene. Calvin has become well-known for the prodigious feat of writing his *Institutes of the Christian Religion* at the age of twenty-six. It was the first really systematic exposition of Reformed theology. Calvin served the church in Strasbourg, France and in Geneva, Switzerland. During these years he made significant contributions to the reform of church worship.

The great Reformer attempted to restore the balance of word and sacrament that was missing in medieval worship. Calvin was convinced that no assembly of the church should be held without the word being preached and the Lord's Supper administered. However, his preference for weekly communion was not approved by the authorities in Geneva so he settled for quarterly observance. He thoroughly rejected the Roman doctrine of transubstantiation and affirmed the real spiritual presence of Christ by faith as the Lord's Supper was celebrated. He thus believed communion to be more than a mere memorial, in contrast to the Zwinglian view.

John Calvin stressed the exposition of Scripture as an essential part of every worship service. He chose to abandon the Roman lectionaries with their prescribed Scripture readings based on the church year calendar. Instead he adopted the *lectio continua* method of reading through whole books of Scripture in consecutive order with faithful expository preaching of the whole counsel of God. John Knox, who spent time with Calvin in Geneva, likewise used the *lectio continua* method of reading and exposition of Scripture in systematic fashion.

Calvin also translated the liturgy into the vernacular and allowed for more congregational participation. His services also included a metrical arrangement of the Psalms for the people to sing. The order of service he used was as follows:

"Our Help is in the name of the Lord"
Confession of sins
Words of pardon
Absolution
Decalogue (sung by congregation)
Prayer for illumination
Lessons from Scripture
Sermon
Offering of alms
Intercessions
Lord's Prayer with paraphrase
Apostles' Creed (sung)
Words of institution
Exhortation
Communion
Post-communion
"Nunc Dimittis" in metre
Benediction

John Calvin's guide in liturgical reform was the regulative principle of worship. He believed in the supreme authority of Scripture and was convinced that true worship is to include only what is authorized by God in his word. Calvin wrote in his *Institutes* concerning the second commandment,

> The purport of the commandment, therefore, is, that he will not have his legitimate worship profaned by superstitious rites. Wherefore, in general, he calls us entirely away from the carnal frivolous observances which our stupid minds are wont to devise after forming some gross idea of the divine nature, while, at the same time, he instructs us in the worship which is legitimate, namely, spiritual worship of his own appointment. (2–VIII:17)

CALVIN

True worship:	False Worship:
What is warranted from Scripture only	Whatever is forbidden or not warranted from Scripture

LUTHER

True worship: False Worship:

What is   Only what is
warranted from   expressly forbidden
Scripture PLUS   by God in Scripture
— — — — — — — — —
Whatever is not
specifically
forbidden

Figure 30:
Calvin and Luther Compared on the Regulative Principle

SURVEY OF THE LITURGICAL CONTRIBUTIONS
OF THE REFORMATION

The Christian church can be eternally grateful to God for raising up men like Zwingli, Luther, Calvin and others who called the church back to its biblical roots. The great Reformation has left an indelible mark that is evident today in churches throughout the world. The contributions of the Reformation to corporate worship may be summarized as follows.

Worship services were once again conducted in the language of the people and in a simplified form that facilitated understanding by the people. Congregational participation in worship was recovered, especially in the singing of Psalms and hymns whereby each believer could exercise his/her priesthood. The important place of the word of God in worship was rethought and the balance between word and sacrament was restored. There was a concern to clearly define the biblical significance of the Lord's Supper. The regulative principle of worship was implemented, thus eliminating numerous accretions that had developed in corporate worship over the years.

How grateful Christians can be for the Reformation. It might be appropriate for you to pause now and thank God for raising up the Reformers. Praise God in prayer for the Reformation. The next time you sing a hymn written by Luther or a Psalm arrangement from Calvin's *Geneva Psalter*, remember the contribution these men made to your worship. It's good to know your roots.

Questions for Review

1. What were some of the problems in the medieval church's worship that called for reformation?

2. Name some contributions that Martin Luther made to the reform of liturgy.

3. Summarize the contributions Ulrich Zwingli made toward reforming the church's worship.

4. What was the medieval *prone*?

5. Name some ways in which John Calvin reformed the liturgy of the church.

6. What were the differences between Calvin's and Luther's views of the regulative principle?

7. Summarize the contributions of the Reformation in the area of church worship.

Questions for Discussion

1. Do you see any problems from the medieval church that still exist and that call for reformation today?

2. What are the main differences today between Lutheran worship and Roman Catholic worship?

3. It is claimed that Zwingli believed worship should appeal to the mind rather than the senses. Do you agree or disagree with Zwingli?

4. In some churches the sermon is looked upon as the real service and all that precedes it is mere preliminaries. What could be done to correct this problem in churches where it exists?

5. What are some of the advantages of using the *lectio continua*

method of reading and expository preaching as Calvin and Knox practiced it?

6. As you look at Calvin's order of worship can you make any observations that might apply to contemporary worshipers?

12

HOW TO ENRICH YOUR CORPORATE WORSHIP

Suggestions are given for the development of one's corporate worshiping muscles as well as ideas on developing enriched private worship.

The popularity of physical fitness is evidenced by the number of people who have become avid devotees of jogging, racquetball, tennis, bicycling and sundry other sports. It takes self-discipline, the sacrifice of time and much effort to develop one's physical fitness, yet many are willing to pay the price to reap the dividends. How many people are as devoted to the development of their worshiping muscles? Worshipers generally need to be taught how to worship. Many have attended church services for years and yet have never developed their worshiping muscles. Several suggestions are given here on how one can develop this capacity and enrich one's corporate worship.

LEARN THE VALUE OF
PRIOR PREPARATION FOR WORSHIP

The early Puritans stressed the inner disciplines of the Christian life including prior heart preparation for services of worship. This preparation meant more than thirty seconds of prayer as one took his place in the pew. For example, the Puritan George Swinnock encouraged private preparation to begin in one's home on Saturday night. He suggested,

Spend some time in consideration of the infinite majesty, holiness, jealousy, and goodness, of that God, with whom thou art to have to do in sacred duties . . . thou canst not think the good thou mayest gain by such forethoughts, how pleasant and profitable a Lord's Day would

121

be to thee after such a preparation. The oven of thine heart thus baked in, as it were, overnight, would be easily heated the next morning; the fire so well raked up when thou wentest to bed, would be sooner kindled when thou shouldest rise. If thou wouldest thus leave thy heart with God on the Saturday night, thou shouldest find it with him in the Lord's Day morning.[1]

This is hardly the way most contemporary Christians spend Saturday evening. Some are up later on Saturday night than any other night of the week and the resulting physical exhaustion takes its toll in the quality of their participation in the service on Sunday morning. The extent of their preparation for worship is limited to the few minutes of the organ prelude and even that time in too many churches is filled with the chattering of garrulous believers about last night's party, Sue's new dress or Bill's promotion. Any opportunity for the living God to speak to them and they to him is lost in the horizontal dialogue. Should not the threshold of corporate worship be prime time for preparation to meet the living God in prayer and in meditation on his word? How helpful it can be to read through the Scripture lessons in advance and to pray specifically that the Lord will receive the praise that he deserves in the service, that he will speak through his word, and that his assembled people will respond to that word with the obedience that glorifies him. It has been suggested that what the church needs in order to deepen corporate worship is not new liturgical forms and gimmicks, but more preparatory "heart work" before using the present forms. If worship is the highest activity of the church and the purpose for which we were created, it certainly deserves one's best in preparatory heart work.

RECOGNIZE THE IMPORTANCE OF A CLEAR CONSCIENCE FOR WORSHIP

The Old Testament priests were required to wash their hands and feet before entering the tabernacle to worship. This preparatory washing took place at a bronze laver which was filled with water and placed near the entrance of the tabernacle. The divine injunction stated: "When they enter the tent of meeting, they shall wash with water, that they may not die; or when they approach to the altar to minister, by offering up in smoke a fire sacrifice to the

Lord. So they shall wash their hands and their feet, that they may not die..." (Exodus 30:20, 21). This represented the need for cleansing before entering the presence of the Holy One. Even today Roman Catholic priests literally wash their hands in a basin of water as part of the mass.

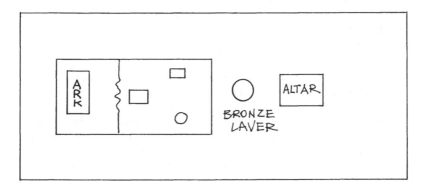

Figure 31:
Washing at the Laver

Your church probably does not have a bronze laver full of water at the entrance, yet there is still a need for a cleansed conscience before worshiping. This cleansing today comes not at the laver but with the confession of sins that are cleansed with the blood of Christ. "Let us draw near [to God] with a sincere heart in full assurance of faith, having our hearts sprinkled clean from an evil conscience and our body washed with pure water" (Hebrews 10:22). The Psalmist asks, "Who may ascend into the hill of the Lord? And who may stand in His holy place? He who has clean hands and a pure heart ..." (Psalm 24:3, 4; cf. Psalm 26:6, 7 and Hebrews 9:14). That Jesus recognized the importance of dealing with sin prior to worship is evident in his instruction, "If therefore you are presenting your offering at the altar, and there remember that your brother has something against you, leave your offering there before the altar, and go your way, first be reconciled to your brother, and then come and present your offering"(Matthew 5:23, 24). It would be difficult to expect to worship if you were not on speaking terms with the person sitting in the pew in front of you.

The resolution of interfering interpersonal friction is a necessary part of the preparation for worship.

Many churches have a prayer of confession at the beginning of the service. Even if your church does not have a formal confession, you can utilize the time during the organ prelude for a silent confession before God so that you may have a cleansed conscience to worship the living God. The *Book of Common Prayer* begins the daily service with this confession:

> Almighty and most merciful Father; We have erred, and strayed from thy ways like lost sheep. We have followed too much the devices and desires of our own hearts. We have offended against thy holy laws. We have left undone those things which we ought to have done; And we have done those things which we ought not to have done; And there is no health in us. But thou, O Lord, have mercy upon us, miserable offenders. Spare thou those, O God, who confess their faults. Restore thou those who are penitent; According to thy promises declared unto mankind in Christ Jesus our Lord. And grant, O most merciful Father, for his sake; That we may hereafter live a godly, righteous, and sober life, To the glory of thy holy Name. Amen.

ENTER WORSHIP SERVICES
EXPECTING TO PARTICIPATE

The scene is an all too common one. You see someone enter a church service and sit as far back as possible in an effort to be inconspicuous. He has had an exhausting week of pressure at the office as well as a late night on Saturday so he wishes to be as undisturbed as possible during the service and to passively watch the action. "Let the minister do the work. After all, isn't that what we pay him for?" This imaginary but all too real Christian is encouraging the atrophy of his worshiping muscles. Jesus Christ "has made us to be a kingdom, priests to His God and Father" (Revelation 1:6). The priesthood of each believer implies one's active participation in worship. One should come with that expectation utilizing an open Bible, the hymnal, a bulletin — and paper and pencil if necessary — to fully enter into the service to God.

Furthermore, one's prime purpose in participating in the service is not to be man-centered but God-centered. The highest motive is not to receive a blessing or to experience some kind of subjective, liver-shivering hallelujah-earthquake that will last until the following Sunday. Rather the prime aim of worshipers should be to give glory to God in response to his revelation of himself. The service should have a dominant Godward focus. Worship then becomes more fulfilling as worshipers unite to actively participate in the offering of praise before the triune God.

RECOGNIZE THE LINK BETWEEN
PRIVATE WORSHIP AND PUBLIC WORSHIP

One cannot isolate private and public worship into separate compartments. As one's private worship develops, one's appreciation for public worship grows, and vice versa.

Figure 32:
The Public/Private Worship Connection

A person who has had a week of vital communion with God will be best prepared to enter into the fullness of corporate praise. Likewise, assembly on the Lord's day can stimulate enriched private devotion during the ensuing week. Each feeds the other.

Several suggestions can be given of ways to enrich one's experience of private worship. You might try reading through a passage of Scripture making a list of all it teaches about the three persons of the Godhead. Then use that list of divine acts and attributes to praise God. Some find it helpful to read a psalm aloud in private and then sing a metrical arrangement of the same psalm. Have you ever used a hymn book in your private worship? Even if a lack of musical aptitude makes singing a painful experience, you can read the words of some of the great worship hymns as expressions of praise to God. Even the occasional use of prayer books has proven helpful to some Christians.

The Psalmist was extremely conscious of the works of creation that reflect the glory of the Creator. For example, in Psalm 148 the whole creation is invoked to praise the Lord:

> Praise the Lord from the earth,
> Sea-monsters and all deeps;
> Fire and hail, snow and clouds;
> Stormy wind, fulfilling His word;
> Mountains and all hills;
> Fruit trees and all cedars
> (vss. 7–9)

Why not allow your exposure to the handiwork of the Creator to inspire praise? In the midst of a thunder storm or walking along the pounding surf of the ocean you can praise God for his majesty and power. Walking under an umbrella in the rain can remind you to thank the Lord for his goodness in blessing the earth with showers. Driving through snow-capped mountains surrounded by picturesque cloud formations can lead to praising the Creator for his eternality and infinity. A sensitivity to the whole splendor of creation can increase your ability to praise God in daily life.

Music can also be used as a stimulus to divine adoration. Try putting Handel's *Dettington Te Deum* on the turntable and then settling back with the stereo headphones. A recording of Bach's *St. Matthew Passion* or *Magnificat* or Handel's famous *Messiah* or Haydn's *Seven Last Words* can prove to be most appropriate Saturday night preparation for Sunday morning worship.

Private worship need not be a spiritually deadening routine performed in a perfunctory manner but can be a rich experience that develops one's appreciation for the fullness of corporate worship. How can you improve your experience of public and private worship? Try filling in the chart below, using the suggestions given throughout this book as well as others that might further prepare you to enter into the future consummated worship before the throne of God.

Amen, blessing and glory and wisdom and thanksgiving and honor and power and might, be to our God forever and ever. Amen. Revelation 7:12

Ways to improve my private worship:	Ways to improve my public worship:

Figure 33:
Improving My Worship

Questions for Review

1. What can contemporary Christians learn from the Puritans about preparation for worship?

2. What are some ways to prepare for corporate worship?

3. Why did the Old Testament priests wash their hands and feet in the laver and what does this say to believers today? (Exodus 30:20, 21; Hebrews 9:14; 10:22; Psalm 24:3, 4; 26:6, 7)

4. What should one expect to happen when one enters a service of worship? (I Peter 2:5; Revelation 1:6)

5. What is the relationship between private and public worship?

Questions for Discussion

1. What suggestions can you give for Saturday activities that would help prepare the heart for Sunday worship?

2. What are the advantages and disadvantages of using public prayers of confession compared to silent prayers of confession?

3. How can churches encourage Christians to come to worship services expecting to participate actively?

4. What are some possible explanations of why some Christians find private worship a spiritually deadening routine?

5. How have you changed through study of this book and what do you plan to do for follow-through?

[1]Cited by James I. Packer, "The Puritan Approach to Worship," *Diversity in Unity*, (London: *The Evangelical Magazine*, 1963), p. 14.

SUGGESTIONS FOR FURTHER READING

DeJong, James A., *Into His Presence: Perspectives on Reformed Worship,* Grand Rapids: Board of Publications of the Christian Reformed Church, 1985.

Edgar, William, *In Spirit and Truth, Ten Bible Studies on Worship,* Downers Grove, Illinois: Inter-Varsity Press, 1976.

Engle, Paul E., *Worship Planbook: A Manual for Worship Leaders,* Philadelphia: Great Commission Publications, 1981.

Mains, Karen Burton, *Making Sunday Special,* Waco, Texas: Word Books, 1987.

Martin, Ralph, *Worship in the Early Church,* Grand Rapids: William B. Eerdmans Publishing Company, 1974.

Maxwell, William D., *A History of Christian Worship,* Grand Rapids: Baker Book House, 1982.

Packer, James I., *Knowing God,* Downers Grove, Illinois: Inter-Varsity Press, 1973.

Rayburn, Robert G., *O Come, Let Us Worship: Corporate Worship in the Evangelical Church,* Grand Rapids: Baker Book House, 1980.